P9-CMR-080

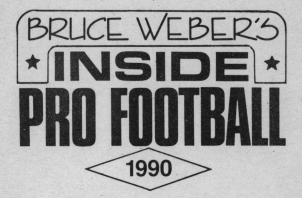

BRUCE WEBER'S
★ INSIDE ★
PRO FOOTBALL
1990

SCHOLASTIC INC.
New York Toronto London Auckland Sydney

For Danny and Arthur Suffin:
May you always be on the winning team.

PHOTO CREDITS:
Cover: Photo of Joe Montana/Focus on Sports. **2, 10, 23, 76:** San Francisco 49ers. **3, 17, 66:** Green Bay Packers. **4, 13, 21, 58:** Philadelphia Eagles. **5, 22, 38:** Cincinnati Bengals. **6, 60:** Washington Redskins. **7, 40:** Houston Oilers. **8, 78:** Los Angeles Rams. **9, 18, 72:** Chicago Bears. **11, 54, 68:** Detroit Lions. **12, 20, 24, 44:** Kansas City Chiefs. **14, 15, 70** (left): Minnesota Vikings. **16, 56:** New York Giants. **19, 46:** Denver Broncos. **26:** Miami Dolphins. **28:** Buffalo Bills. **30:** New England Patriots. **32:** Indianapolis Colts. **34:** New York Jets. **36:** Pittsburgh Steelers. **42:** Cleveland Browns. **48:** Los Angeles Raiders. **50:** San Diego Chargers. **52:** Seattle Seahawks. **62, 70** (right): Dallas Cowboys. **64:** Phoenix Cardinals. **74:** Tampa Bay Buccaneers. **80:** Atlanta Falcons. **82:** New Orleans Saints. **84:** University of Illinois Sports Information/Photo by Mark Jones.

ISBN 0-590-43464-0

12 11 10 9 8 7 6 5 4 3 2 1   0 1 2 3 4 5/9

Printed in the U.S.A.   01

First Scholastic printing, September 1990

CONTENTS

INTRODUCTION
The Team of the Nineties?

It began just moments after the San Francisco 49ers had finished demolishing the Denver Broncos last January. The Bay Area bombers' 55–10 blowout left no doubt about the team of the eighties. With four Super Bowl titles in the decade, the Niners were easily the class of the era. The next question: Who will be the team of the nineties?

Within months, every team came up a winner. For the next four years, the new five-network TV deal puts $32 million per year in every owner's pocket. So the team of the nineties must be commissioner Paul Tagliabue and his TV negotiations committee.

But championships are decided on the field. So let's look beyond money. Some folks believe the 49ers will continue to dominate — and they may, though no team has ever won three straight Super Bowls. Coach George Seifert has managed to carry on in the best Bill Walsh tradition. The front office seems to come up with the players to get it done. And owner Eddie DeBartolo is so good to his players that none of them want to leave.

San Francisco's biggest challenge could come within its own division, the NFC West. The supremely well coached Los Angeles Rams, blessed with an outstanding young QB in Jim Everett, should continue to press the Niners. New Orleans has a championship defense but a questionable offense, unless coach Jim Mora can solve his QB problems. Atlanta enters the sometimes wonderful, often wacky world of Jerry Glanville. The three-for-one deal for the top '90 draft choice should bolster the longtime doormat Falcons.

Quarterbacking, advancing years, and killer injuries may have ended the dominating years of the Chicago Bears. The Minnesota Vikings' personnel is as good as anyone's, though putting it all together seems beyond the reach of coach Jerry Burns and staff. The Lions may finally shed their pussycat image. Barry Sanders *is* the real thing, and No. 1 draftee Andre Ware may be. They can make the high-risk run-and-shoot offense pay off big-time. If the Lions don't roar, Green Bay may be next in line. The Pack hasn't been heard from since Super Bowls I and II, but they could be back by XXVI or XXVII. Tampa Bay should be much improved, particularly if Keith McCants is as good as he seemed to be last February or March.

The Dallas Cowboys are on their way back, but after a 1–15 record, it's a long way. The Cardinals don't seem to be making progress, which isn't thrilling the folks in Phoenix. The Giants and Eagles are both carefully built and rebuilt, each with weaknesses that they seem to be able to mask. The Washington Redskins have the tools to catch the front-runners, though it might not happen in 1990 or 1991.

The AFC, bruised and battered after a series of Super Bowl blowouts, believes that the nineties, like the seventies, can be its decade. The Indianapolis Colts have given up a pile of talent for a few stars (and potential future stars like Jeff George) and may challenge the Buffalo Bills in the East. The Jets are rebuilding (their draft was excellent), the Dolphins are retooling (the defense is better), and the Patriots are reloading (if they can stay healthy).

The Central Division is the AFC's toughest. Three of the four teams (Cleveland, Pittsburgh, Houston) went to the play-offs last season; the fourth (Cincinnati) had been to the Super Bowl the previous year.

Seemingly unbeatable at home, the Denver Broncos win frequent trips to the Super Bowl. After losing by a combined 126–40 score on the last three Super visits, some Bronco fans may not even watch if the team makes it to Tampa next January. While the San Diego Chargers and Kansas City Chiefs seem to be headed in the right direction, the Broncos' other rivals, the Raiders and Seahawks, seem to be standing still — and that's being kind.

Thanks to the 17-week schedule this year (it goes to 18 next year), you'll see more NFL football than ever before (at least 95 regular-season games in most TV markets, if you've got cable). Overkill? Forget it. Sit back and enjoy!

— Bruce Weber

•

National Football League All-Pro Team

Wide Receiver
JERRY RICE
SAN FRANCISCO 49ERS

Most experts concede that the 49ers' Joe Montana is football's best quarterback. Since Joe can't throw the ball to himself, that speaks volumes for Jerry Rice.

A one-time legend at tiny Mississippi Valley College, Rice is blessed with the two skills that make for a great receiver: excellent hands and superb speed. Most importantly, he can make things happen anytime he gets his hands on the ball.

Ask the New York Giants. During the '88 season, the Giants had an early-season victory over the Niners all but wrapped up. San Fran was mired deep in their territory. They were practically out of time. Then Rice split two defenders and picked off a perfect Montana toss. The rest, as they say, is history. No one catches Rice from behind.

The MVP of Super Bowl XXIII when his late-game heroics led to the winning TD against Cincinnati, Rice was just as impressive in Super Bowl XXIV when the Niners blew away the Denver Broncos.

His 82 catches last season produced league-high totals of 1,483 yards and 17 TDs, just off his 1986 career-best 86 catches and 1,570 yards. With four straight 1,000-yard seasons behind him, Rice continues to prove that he's No. 1.

Wide Receiver
STERLING SHARPE
GREEN BAY PACKERS

The folks in Green Bay think their man Sterling Sharpe has a lot of Magic Johnson in him. Both of them smile a lot and both of them can do incredible things with a ball. Of course, the Packers have their own Magic man, QB Don Majkowski. He'll be the first to tell you what Sharpe means to him.

Sharpe arrived in Wisconsin after a stellar career at South Carolina. The Pack's first-round draft pick (the seventh player selected) in 1988, he was an instant success. Injuries to Phil Epps and Walter Stanley forced him into the lineup, and he responded with a team-leading (and Packer rookie-record) 55 catches. The smile was always there — and for good reason.

Then in '89 Sharpe blew the whole league away. His 90 catches led the NFL. He picked up 1,423 yards (a 15.8 yards-per-catch average) and scored 12 TDs (including one for 79 yards). It was no accident that the longtime doormat Pack went 10–6, the same record as NFC Central leader Minnesota.

Some critics aren't fond of Sharpe's happy-go-lucky attitude. Sterling doesn't agree, of course. "Sure it's a job, but it's a job I've always dreamed of," he says. "As long as I'm here, I want to enjoy every minute."

Tight End
KEITH JACKSON
PHILADELPHIA EAGLES

About the only thing that can stop the Philadelphia Eagles' Keith Jackson is an injury. The former Oklahoma U. All-America suffered with back spasms, a twisted knee, and a sprained ankle that kept him out of all or part of eight games last season. Still in '89 he pulled in 63 passes for 648 yards — and even scored three TDs in one incredible come-from-behind 42–37 victory against Washington.

That was good enough to lead all NFL tight ends in receiving and to earn him his second straight start in the Pro Bowl, election to the All-Pro and All-Madden teams, and the tight-end spot on the Eagles' All-Eighties team after only two seasons.

The 6–2, 250-pounder is simply the perfect TE. He catches like a wide receiver, runs like a back, and blocks like a tackle.

"I like to be different," says Jackson, who plays the cello, owns a one-of-a-kind clothing store, and earned his college degree in only 3½ years. That's fine with the Eagles, who made Jackson their No. 1 draft pick in '88, though he caught only 13 passes during his senior college season for the run-happy Sooners. But his career average of 23.7 yards per catch convinced the Eagles that he was the real thing.

4

Offensive Tackle
ANTHONY MUNOZ
CINCINNATI BENGALS

Is Anthony Munoz the best offensive tackle in football? Just ask his coach, Sam Wyche. "That's not even close," says the Bengal boss. "I believe he is the greatest offensive tackle in football history."

A lot of folks in the NFL agree. Despite crippling injuries that might have stopped lesser men, the 10-year veteran continues to excel in every phase of the game — run-blocking, pass protection, even catching an occasional tackle-eligible pass.

Last January, Munoz was selected for his ninth straight Pro Bowl. He was the first offensive lineman ever to accomplish that. (Other nine-timers include DT Randy White, RB Franco Harris, and LBs Lawrence Taylor and Jack Lambert.)

At 6–6 and 278 pounds, Munoz is certainly blessed with good tackle size. But size alone (there are bigger tackles) doesn't get it done. Basically Munoz is an outstanding athlete. Combined with 10 years of experience at age 31, Anthony cannot be outthought, outfought, or outquicked. There isn't a defensive end alive who looks forward to facing Anthony Munoz.

The best offensive tackle ever? Old-timers may disagree, but Munoz is right up there with the all-time best.

JIM LACHEY
WASHINGTON REDSKINS

The Chargers and Raiders must be kicking themselves. San Diego dealt Jim Lachey to Al Davis's team (for practically nothing) in 1988. Then the Raiders, groping for a quarterback, sent the former Ohio State star to the Redskins for Jay Schroeder a few weeks later. Now Schroeder spends as much time on the Raiders' bench as he does in the Raiders' huddle while Lachey is a sure-fire All-Pro.

"We knew Jim was good," said Washington coach Joe Gibbs this spring. "We just didn't know how good. He was great last season. Jim should be an All-Pro for the rest of his NFL career."

The Skins' NFC rivals know how tough the 6–6, 290-pounder is. Against the Giants' Lawrence Taylor in Game 6 last season, Lachey allowed L.T. only one unassisted and two assisted tackles. Against the Bears' Richard Dent, he didn't allow a single tackle.

"It was no accident that our line allowed the second fewest sacks in the league [21]," says Gibbs. "Lachey is one of our team leaders and one of the two top tackles in the NFL. Despite injuries [bruised shoulder, dislocated thumb] and a changing cast of linemates, he gets the job done every week."

Guard
BRUCE MATTHEWS
HOUSTON OILERS

When Houston center Jay Pennison and backup George Yarno went down with injuries late in the '89 season, then-coach Jerry Glanville never hesitated. He pointed to All-Pro guard Bruce Matthews and, for the first time in five years, Matthews became the Oiler pivot man.

Positions may change, but the results don't. The Matthews-led line didn't allow a single sack of QB Warren Moon, one of six sackless games last year.

The rugged 6–5, 293-pounder is there every week for the Oilers. In his 104 NFL games, he has been the starter 100 times. Veteran Houston watchers point to Matthews (and his guard partner, Mike Munchak) as the keys to the Oilers' potent offense. When the chips were down in the final game last season, with the play-offs on the line, Houston came up with 483 yards of offense. Great offensive lines make that happen.

Matthews is a member of one of the NFL's best families. He and brother Clay (a Cleveland LB) played in the 1989 Pro Bowl, the first same-time brother act in the long history of that post-season "classic." The Cunninghams, Sam and Randall, had pulled the trick previously — nine years apart.

7

TOM NEWBERRY
LOS ANGELES RAMS

For as long as most football folks can remember, the Rams have been blessed with at least one All-Pro-type offensive guard. But when Dennis Harrah retired, it looked like the tradition would end.

Enter Tom Newberry. The 6-2, 285-pounder was a late-bloomer. Not too many All-Pros come out of Wisconsin-LaCrosse. But the Rams knew he was something special. They picked him in the second round of the 1986 draft, and it paid off immediately. Newberry stepped into the L.A. starting lineup during his third game and has started the last 58 games — and the last two Pro Bowls! Barring injury, he'll be there a lot longer.

"He's so tough," raves Rams' boss John Robinson. "Tom is a guard who is a nose tackle at heart. Lots of linemen are good on the run, weak on pass protection. Others are poor blockers and super protectors. Tom is both. That's what makes him so valuable."

As the Rams begin to rebuild their aging offensive line (three starters are 32 or older), they'll build around Tom Newberry. Once a world-class shot-putter (ranked eighth in the world in '85), Tom is a superb building block(er).

Center
JAY HILGENBERG
CHICAGO BEARS

Chicago Bear fans probably think that Jay Hilgenberg's last name is "Playing Hurt." The Bears' center has started 100 straight games and played in 133 in a row, tops on the team, despite injuries that would send most humans scrambling for the injured-reserve list. And he's done it well enough to earn five straight trips to the Pro Bowl.

"It's impossible to tell how good he'd be if he was healthy," says coach Mike Ditka. "It looks like he'll be in better shape for 1990 than he has been in years. And that's great. He's a true pro — and certainly he's one of the leaders on our offense."

The 6–2, 260-pounder comes from a long line of tough linemen. His uncle Wally was a star Viking linebacker. His dad was an All-America center for Iowa in the fifties. And his brothers Jim and Joel (now with the New Orleans Saints) played center for the Hawkeyes before and after Jay did.

The growth of three-man defensive lines, which place a noseman right in front of the center, makes the position more difficult than ever. But despite a dislocated elbow, torn rotator cuff, and other killer injuries, rugged Jay Hilgenberg does it better than anyone.

Quarterback
JOE
MONTANA
SAN FRANCISCO 49ERS

The Quarterback of the Nineties — the early nineties at least — is the Quarterback of the Eighties. There's no doubt that Joe Montana is the most frightening QB in the NFL. One question: Is he the best ever?

The 1979 third-round draft choice from Notre Dame continues to amaze wise football watchers — and players. "I can't believe him," says Niner linebacker Keena Turner. "It's a thrill just watching him work."

Montana operates with the skill of a surgeon, finding tiny holes in the defense. And he rarely makes a mistake. His 1989 passing rating (112.4, whatever that means) was 20 points better than runner-up Boomer Esiason. Only 15 points separated the next 10 QBs. More impressively, Montana hit on 70.2% of his passes, threw only eight interceptions in 386 attempts, and passed for 26 TDs.

Everyone saw Joe pick apart the Bronco defense, 55–10, for his fourth Super Bowl title in the last nine games. That wasn't as impressive as his early-season victory over the Eagles. Trailing 28–17 with 8:24 to go and with Reggie White and his friends in his face, Montana rallied his troops with three quick TDs for a 38–28 win.

The best ever? Just could be.

Running Back
BARRY SANDERS
DETROIT LIONS

Barring injury, Barry Sanders could well be the All-Pro running back right into the 21st century. The former Oklahoma State star, who bolted for the NFL after his Heisman-winning junior year, thrilled the longtime doormat Lions and scared the daylights out of regular Lion-beaters.

"He's as good as anyone I've seen," said Chicago's Mike Ditka, who coached a fairly good runner named Walter Payton. Payton is even more objective. "He's better than I was," says the retired Bear.

Lion fans believe that Barry is the real thing and could finally make the Lions winners. In the last 32 years, Detroit has won exactly zero play-off games and only one division title.

At only 5–8 and 203 pounds, Sanders's talent arrives in an unusual package. His legs look more like a tackle's, which gives him outstanding balance and starting speed. That combination, plus a superb ability to run in traffic, gave him 1,470 yards and 14 TDs last season.

Coach Wayne Fontes is delighted with the prospect of having Barry leading his offense for the next decade. "We have to put the ball in his hands, running and passing, at least 30 times a game," says Fontes.

Running Back
CHRISTIAN OKOYE
KANSAS CITY CHIEFS

In one short season, the Kansas City Chiefs' running back Christian Okoye went from a broadcasters' nightmare to The Nigerian Nightmare. The men with the microphones couldn't decide how to say the 6–1, 255-pounder's name. (Christian prefers ah-COY-ya.) Kaycee opponents, of course, don't have that problem. Theirs is trying to tackle the huge, quick Okoye, a much more difficult task.

Incredibly, Okoye has been playing football for only seven years. Though he had never played organized football before, the native of Enugu, Nigeria, decided to try out for his college team at Azusa Pacific in California. He was an instant hit. Four seasons later, he became the Chiefs' second-round draft pick.

Despite his inexperience, Christian gained 660 rushing yards in his rookie year. After injuries held him to 473 in his second year, he finally blossomed last season. His 370 carries and 1,480 yards both led the NFL. And his crunching blocks gave Kaycee's quarterbacks plenty of time to throw.

Coach Marty Schottenheimer thinks his star runner will only get better. "He wants to improve and he can," says Schottenheimer. "No one will outwork him."

12

Defensive End
REGGIE WHITE
PHILADELPHIA EAGLES

When Reggie White, the NFL's Minister of Defense, teaches his Sunday School classes or preaches at churches throughout the U.S., the 6–5, 285-pound Baptist minister inspires. On the football field, the Philadelphia Eagles' DE merely frightens.

The deeply religious White is, according to his coach, Buddy Ryan, "the best I've ever been around." Okay, Buddy may be biased. Mike Ditka isn't. The Bear boss says, "If there's a better defensive end than Reggie, I haven't seen him."

The one-time U. of Tennessee All-America spent his first pro season with the USFL's Memphis Showboats, then moved on to Philly for the 1985 season. He's such an awesome figure on the gridiron that Eagle opponents plan their entire pass-protection game to stop him. Limited to a career-low 11 sacks in '89, his presence enabled his teammate Clyde Simmons to register 15 sacks. That's impact.

"My whole objective in playing football is to set an example for young people," says White. "If I can help someone, then I've done something important."

What he's doing is also important enough to merit a $1.5-million-per-year salary from the Eagles. That's not too shabby either.

13

CHRIS DOLEMAN
MINNESOTA VIKINGS

It has happened before. When Randy White came out of the University of Maryland, the Dallas Cowboys figured he'd be the greatest linebacker who ever lived. They were dead wrong. Moved to defensive tackle, White became a regular member of the All-Pro team.

Minnesota made the same mistake with Chris Doleman. A star at the U. of Pittsburgh, Doleman immediately moved in as a LB. He wasn't bad, but he didn't make anyone forget Lawrence Taylor either. Then the Vikes moved Doleman to defensive end. He was an instant success.

At 6–5 and 260 pounds, Doleman has all the tools: speed, strength, quickness, football intelligence. He and defensive tackle Keith Millard give the Vikes an enormous one-two punch on the defensive line. If the defense gangs up on Chris, Keith gets the QB from the inside. When they concentrate on Millard, Doleman zips up the field to capture the passer.

"Chris is a great team player," says coach Jerry Burns. "As quick as he is on the pass-rush, he still plays the run extremely well, always staying in his lanes. You couldn't ask for anyone better at defensive end." Viking opponents agree.

Defensive Tackle
KEITH MILLARD
MINNESOTA VIKINGS

Preparing to play the Minnesota Vikings must be a quarterback's worst nightmare. Defensive tackle Keith Millard and defensive end Chris Doleman make a living wrecking passers and passing games.

Millard's strength and quickness make him an absolute terror on the pass-rush. A one-time Jacksonville Bull of the old USFL, Keith arrived in Minnesota in time for the 1985 season. He led the team that season (with 11 sacks) and three times in his first four years. In '89, the 27-year-old Millard led the league in sacks for most of the season before a shoulder separation slowed him in December. Still he finished with 18 (an amazing total for a tackle), along with 90 tackles (70 solos), an interception, and a TD on a fumble recovery.

What makes Millard so good? He's quick and he's intense. It's a great combination. San Francisco coach George Seifert points to Millard's quick moves. "He's very strong off the ball," says Seifert, "and then he explodes into the backfield."

"You have to be impressed with how Keith plays in pain," says Viking general manager Mike Lynn. "And he's a team man all the way. Individual accomplishments don't mean a thing to Keith."

Outside Linebacker
LAWRENCE TAYLOR
NEW YORK GIANTS

Every time some hotshot college linebacker prepares to move to the NFL, the scouts all declare him "the next Lawrence Taylor." (Alabama's Keith McCants is the latest addition to the next-Taylor group.)

Meanwhile no one has managed to outdo the original. That's why we'll start the nineties just as we ended the eighties, with the Giants' madman as our All-Pro outside LB.

Though a broken ankle, which would have ended most players' seasons, cost L.T. two games last year, the former U. of North Carolina star still managed a routine-for-him 15 sacks a year ago. That helped his Giants hold their opponents to just under 16 points per game, second best in the NFL.

Most coaches rate the Giants' LBs as the best unit in the league. That simply couldn't happen without Taylor. Even after nine body-bruising years, the 6–3, 243-pound L.T. still commands considerable attention from opposing offenses. The speed, quickness, amazing strength, and unbelievable intensity that have marked his career are still there, with some still to spare. How long he can keep up the pace is a question Giant GM George Young and coach Bill Parcells don't want to think about!

Outside Linebacker
TIM HARRIS
GREEN BAY PACKERS

If Tim Harris ever wins an NFL popularity contest, you'll know that the Packers stuffed the ballot box. The Pack sack-maker (only Minnesota's Chris Doleman had more) became the first Green Bay defensive Pro Bowler in a decade.

"Timmy makes all of us better," says his LB mate Brian Noble. "He's beating up the other guys on every play. That makes it a lot easier for us." Harris led the team in forced fumbles (four) and fumbles recovered (tied with three). A great pass-rusher, his hard work has paid off against the run.

How important is Tim to the Packer defense? Catch these numbers. He accounted for 19½ of the team's 34 sacks. That's 57.4% of the Pack's total. No one else in the league came close.

Green Bay defensive coordinator Hank Bullough knows what to do with Harris. Anything Tim wants! He lines up anywhere he thinks he can get to the quarterback. Atlanta's Mike Kenn found out how dangerous that can be. Harris got four sacks against him. He beat Detroit's Eric Sanders three times.

Blessed with great strength, quick hands, and decent speed, Tim should continue to make Pack rivals miserable every Sunday.

Inside Linebacker
MIKE SINGLETARY
CHICAGO BEARS

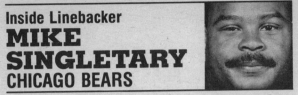

It was the worst of times in Chicago last season. The awesome Bears played like little teddies, went 6–10, and finished fourth in the NFC Central. But while injuries and breakdowns were ruining his club, inside 'backer Mike Singletary stood tall and strong.

"Mike is the key man on our team," says coach Mike Ditka. "He is what's best about football. We're blessed to have him. I wouldn't trade him for anyone."

The one-time Baylor star has simply made himself the best at his position. He isn't the biggest, strongest, or fastest. He just works harder and plays smarter than anyone else.

Years ago, Singletary decided that the best way to lead was by example. And he has done just that. Off the field and on the field — on practice days and game days — the 225-pounder is the glue that holds the club together. As team captain, he takes charge, working especially well with the younger Bears. His pregame preparation through careful film study is well known.

"I try to outthink the opponents," says Singletary. "I figure out what they're going to do against our personnel and plan to stop them."

Inside Linebacker
KARL
MECKLENBURG
DENVER BRONCOS

For years Karl Mecklenburg was the Denver defense. You never knew where the 6–3, 240-pounder would line up. He might be at defensive end, at tackle, at inside linebacker, at outside linebacker. Anywhere. And he was superb. Three times in his first four seasons, he made the AFC Pro Bowl team.

Trouble was, Denver's defense wasn't very good. Don't blame the former Minnesota U. star. His teammates just didn't measure up.

Enter Wade Phillips, one of the NFL's top defensive coordinators (and a near-future head coach). Denver boss Dan Reeves gave him the job of turning around the Bronco unit. (Forget the Super Bowl!) His first move was installing Mecklenburg at inside linebacker — and only inside linebacker.

The results: another Pro Bowl start, Defensive Player of the Month (November), 143 team-leading tackles, a 23-yard fumble return for his first pro TD, and 7½ sacks. He also recovered three other fumbles, forced two more, and defensed three passes.

It was the kind of super year that NFL insiders knew Mecklenburg would turn in. He'll do it again in '90.

ALBERT LEWIS

KANSAS CITY CHIEFS

Despite rather lean years for the team, the Kansas City secondary has always been solid. Lloyd Buruss and Deron Cherry were frequent All-Pros. Now it's cornerback Albert Lewis who is the most fearsome Chief.

Most Sundays, coach Marty Schottenheimer just picks out the opponents' top receiver and tells Lewis to shut him out. Last December, for example, when the Chiefs visited Green Bay, Lewis got Sterling Sharpe, who finished the season with 90 receptions, tops in the NFL. How did he do against Lewis? One catch for five yards. The result: a rare 21–3 road victory for Kaycee.

A one-time seventh round draft choice, the seven-year veteran Lewis had only four interceptions for the Chiefs in '89. Why didn't he have more? Simply because opposing quarterbacks quickly learned not to throw anywhere in Lewis's neighborhood. Still he managed to tie for the team lead in INTs, lead with 17 pass deflections, and chip in with 57 tackles.

The three-time Pro Bowler doesn't go off duty on fourth-and-long either. A terror on special teams, Lewis blocked another punt last season, the sixth of his stellar career.

Cornerback
ERIC ALLEN
PHILADELPHIA EAGLES

As a rookie from Arizona State in 1988, the Philadelphia Eagles' Eric Allen got quite an education. Coach Buddy Ryan's attack defense was based on safety blitzes, line-backer blitzes, rushing linemen. As a result, the young cornerback often found himself surrounded by enemy receivers. He got burned — fairly often.

A compact 5–10, 188-pounder, Allen learned well to deal with an Eagle CB's problems. "He's smart," says coach Ryan. "Even better, he's fast and tough. That's what our defense needs to succeed."

NFL quarterbacks like the Giants' Phil Simms and the Broncos' John Elway learned how good Eric had become in his second year. The bigger the game, the better Eric played in '89. His eight interceptions led the NFC. Only Cleveland's Felix Wright had more (nine).

NFL defensive coaches readily admit that cornerback is the toughest position. The CB is always exposed, particularly in the Eagles' scheme of things. But Allen seems to have it under control. He's just about the best cover man in the league. "His main job," says Ryan, "is to prevent the comple-tion. But if we get enough pressure up front, he can do even more."

21

DAVID FULCHER

CINCINNATI BENGALS

Catch David Fulcher in the Bengals' locker room and you think you're looking at a linebacker. Why not? He has linebacker size: 6–3 and 235 pounds. But the NFL's biggest defensive back is also among its best. And no one does the job at strong safety like the former Arizona State star.

"Sure, he's big," says Bengal coach Sam Wyche. "But that's not important. What's important is that he can flat-out play."

The four-year veteran was never better than in the 1989 season. Remember Cincy's 61–7 pasting of the Houston Oilers? Give lots of credit to Fulcher, who merely intercepted three passes and recovered a fumble to lead a Bengal rout.

Fulcher wound up the season with eight INTs, trailing only Cleveland's Felix Wright (nine). He was also the Bengals' tackling leader. Thanks to his size, he's a mighty force on a safety blitz. "Most teams have to protect a blitzing safety," says Cincy defensive coordinator Dick LeBeau. "Not us. David can do the job on his own, freeing us to use our linebackers in pass coverage. It's a key advantage for us. His size and ability enable us to use him in so many different packages, sort of a half safety, half linebacker. He's a tremendous asset."

Free Safety
RONNIE LOTT
SAN FRANCISCO 49ERS

Ask most people to identify the keys to the success of the two-time Super Bowl champion 49ers and you'll quickly get answers like Joe Montana and Jerry Rice. You might even get a vote or two for ex-coach Bill Walsh and new coach George Seifert. Insiders will tell you, however, that free safety Ronnie Lott is the guy who gets the 49ers going.

A 1981 first-round draft pick from Southern Cal (only Montana and Keena Turner have been Niners longer), Lott is the defensive big-play man. Despite missing five weeks last year with an ankle injury, Lott bounced back to steer San Fran into and through the 1989–90 play-offs. At age 31 (last May), the 6-0, 200-pounder is just as tough, just as quick as ever.

The bigger the game, the bigger Ronnie plays. In a late-season contest with the Giants, he had six solo tackles. In the opening play-off game against Minnesota, he had three tackles, one defensed pass, a forced fumble (that he recovered), and a 58-yard TD on an interception. In the NFC finals against the Rams, it was four tackles, an interception, and a key TD-saving breakup.

That's a typical day's work for Lott.

The Nigerian Nightmare, Christian Okoye, figures to have his Kansas City Chiefs in the hunt for the 1990 AFC West title.

American Football Conference Team Previews

AFC East
MIAMI DOLPHINS
1989 Finish: Second (tied)
1990 Prediction: First

Barry Krauss   **Sammie Smith**

Hard to believe, but Miami QB Dan Marino hasn't been to the play-offs since 1985. About the best news for the man with the golden gun is that nobody in the AFC East is on the verge of becoming a super power.

The NFL's winningest coach, Don Shula, was pleased with his team's improvement from 6–10 to 8–8 last year. But, he said, "we just didn't get it done." The Dolphins had been 7–4 and a play-off lock before fading during the final five weeks.

Marino, who wouldn't mind a trade that would take him to a contender, had 24 TDs and 3,997 yards in '89 despite nagging injuries and no running game. His backup, strong-armed Scott Secules, waits.

The nonrunning running game has potential with '89 rookie Sammie Smith (200 for 659), who must learn to take the hard NFL hits and catch the ball more often. Troy Stradford tries to return from serious knee surgery. The FB spot (five different Fish started in '89) needs major upgrading.

The Marks Brothers (leading catcher Mark Clayton with 64 for 1,011 and Mark Duper with 49 for 717) should return to their old spots, joining everybody's backup Jim Jensen (61 for 557) and young Andre Brown. TE Ferrell Edmonds (32 for 382) made the Pro Bowl, though he still has a way to go.

The offensive line is a major problem. Miami will build around young C Jeff Uhlenhake. Starting RT Ronnie Lee and backups Louis Cheek and Tom Toth all left as Plan B's. T Jeff Dellenbach and Gs Roy Foster and Harry Galbreath should return. Top picks T Richmond Webb and G Keith Sims will help.

There's renewed hope on Miami's in-and-out defense. If LILB John Offerdahl is ready and happy, it should be more in than out. RILB Barry Krauss was a happy surprise in '89 (119 tackles in 12 full games), but he and mates E.J. Junior and Hugh Green are getting old. Eric Kumerow must be ready to step in quickly.

It's the same story at CB, where Paul Lankford hangs out. Plan B pickup Donnie Elder may help. Louis Oliver will be a fine FS soon; ex-49er Tim McKyer is super.

T.J. Turner and Jeff Cross figure to bookend Brian Sochia on the defensive line. PK Pete Stoyanovich had a fine rookie season.

AFC East
BUFFALO BILLS
1989 Finish: First
1990 Prediction: Second

Jim Kelly   **Shane Conlan**

Despite an AFC East title, the Buffalo Bills took a giant step backward from a Super Bowl trip last season. A year that started on a high note ended in a flood of losses and hot tempers. Can coach Marv Levy (or all the king's men) put the Bills together again?

Unpopular with fans and some teammates for criticizing Bill players to the press, QB Jim Kelly (228 completions of 391 passes, 3,130 yards, 25 TDs) remains a major talent at QB. Still, he cannot maintain his effectiveness as a leader if he continues to knock others in public. Backup Frank Reich, who got his first serious action last season when Kelly separated a shoulder, went 3–0 before returning to the bench.

RB Thurman Thomas was merely super

in '89, with 298 carries for 1,244 yards and 6 TDs, along with 60 receptions for another 669 yards and 6 more scores. Larry Kinnebrew, Kenneth Davis, and Jamie Mueller provide excellent depth.

WR Andre Reed (88 catches for 1,312 yards, 9 TDs) is among the class of the league, but there's not enough speed from mates James Lofton and Don Beebe or huge TE Pete Metzelaars (6–7, 250).

C Kent Hull is the hub of the offensive front, leading Ts Will Wolford and Howard Ballard and G Jim Ritcher. But who will replace departed vet RG Joe Devlin?

The defense was a major disappointment for the Bills last year. It could get worse. Starting DE Art Still and NT Fred Smerlas are gone, leaving underachiever DRE Bruce Smith and possible replacements in DE Leon Seals and NT Jeff Wright.

Linebacking is Buffalo's pride and joy. The left side of Cornelius Bennett and Shane Conlan may be the NFL's best pair. But ROLB Darryl Talley (97 tackles, 2 blocked kicks) may have been even better in '89.

The secondary has more than its share of problems. FS Mark Kelso is probably too slow, and LCB Kirby Jackson may not be good enough. Both SS Leonard Smith, a former All-Pro, and RCB Nate Odomes are solid. Top pick CB J.D. Williams fits well.

In an exchange of Plan B's, P Rick Tuten may replace departed John Kidd. PK Scott Norwood enjoyed a fine '89.

AFC East
NEW ENGLAND PATRIOTS
1989 Finish: Fourth
1990 Prediction: Third

Eric Sievers   Brent Williams

They'll be selling tons of programs at the Patriots' Sullivan Stadium this fall. Think of the new faces. Dick Steinberg left to become the front-office leader of the Jets. Coach Ray Berry was canned, replaced by Rod Rust. Seventeen players, including several 1989 starters, left via the Plan B door. No one in the NFL lost more. But 11 new faces showed up at the same door, led by three ex-New York Giant starters.

The Pats' '89 campaign ended before it began. All-Pro LB Andre Tippett, top-notch DE Garin Veris, and starting CB Ronnie Lippett all went down for the season during the final quarter of the last preseason game. The return of that trio alone should make '90 better.

None of them will solve the QB situation, however. Aging Steve Grogan (133 of 261, 1,697 yards, 9TDs) should get the nod, with Marc Wilson (75 of 150, 1,006 yards, 3 TDs) behind him. Neither fires the imagination.

The running game will be decent if John Stephens (244 carries for 833 yards) is healthy, which he usually is. Ex-Redskin Jamie Morris and ex-Giant George Adams will get long looks in New England, joining FB Robert Perryman.

When a backup TE and WR like Eric Sievers (54 catches for 615 yards) is your No. 1 receiver, it can spell trouble. But the Pats are in good shape with Cedric Jones, Irving Fryar, Hart Lee Dykes, and a healthy Stanley Morgan. TE could be a problem, unless ex-Giant Zeke Mowatt is ready.

New England will have to replace C Mike Baab (Bob White?), though Ts Danny Villa and Bruce Armstrong and Gs Sean Farrell and Paul Fairchild are strong.

The return of DE Veris and No. 2 pick Ray Agnew bolsters the defensive front, where aging Ken Sims and Brent Williams and NT Tim Goad hung on last year. LB Tippett rejoins Pro Bowler Johnny Rembert, Ed Reynolds, Vincent Brown, and top pick Chris Singleton.

The secondary, long a Patriot strength, has become a question mark. If LCB Lippett returns healthy, so much the better, because RCB Ray Clayborn bolted for Cleveland. SS Roland James and FS Fred Marion have both slipped a bit.

AFC East
INDIANAPOLIS COLTS
1989 Finish: Second (tied)
1990 Prediction: Fourth

Duane Bickett   **O'Brien Alston**

At the end of the '89 season, Indianapolis coach Ron Meyer stated flatly, "We're right where we were a year ago." Most NFL experts disagree; the Colts seemed to take a couple of steps backward. Either way, the now-.500 team has some major questions entering 1990.

Tops among them is Eric Dickerson, who cost the team a bundle of draft picks in '87. The goggled RB (314 carries, 1,311 yards, 8 TDs) wanted (1) more money, (2) a new offensive line, (3) a trade, (4) more money, and/or (5) retirement. If Dickerson disappears, look for Albert Bentley (75 for 299) to do a decent job.

If expensive top pick Jeff George is ready, he'll start. If not, if Chris Chandler is fully recovered (knee surgery), he'll probably regain his QB job from Jack Trudeau (190 for 362, 2,317 yards, 15 TDs), who played most of '89 in great pain.

Speedy rookie Andre Rison (52 catches, 820 yards, 4 TDs) was dealt to Atlanta for George. Bill Brooks caught 63 for 919 yards last year. TE Pat Beach (only 14 catches) isn't fast enough. Could be trouble!

Look for changes on the offensive line. RG Ben Utt bolted for Atlanta via the Plan B route. C Ray Donaldson has slipped, and RT Kevin Call has been bombarded with injuries. Pro Bowl LT Chris Hinton is off to Atlanta in the George deal, but LG Randy Dixon has worlds of potential.

Look for Mitchell Benson to push NT Harvey Armstrong on the defensive front. DRE Jon Hand returns from his finest pro season (10 sacks, 4 forced fumbles, 7 QB hurries). DLE Donnell Thompson is solid.

If O'Brien Alston makes it back from the injured list, the Colts will be overloaded at OLB. Chip Banks, Duane Bickett, and Quintus McDonald provide quite a cushion. Ex-Seahawk Fredd Young and Jeff Herrod are fine inside.

The secondary is adequate, with John Baylor and Eugene Daniel on the corners, Michael Ball at SS, and Mike Prior at FS. A superback could take the whole group another notch, but the Colts seem satisfied with what they have.

Special teams are more than satisfying. The Colts' combo of P Rohn Stark and PK Dean Biasucci (21 of 27 FGs) is terrific.

AFC East
NEW YORK JETS
1989 Finish: Fifth
1990 Prediction: Fifth

Al Toon   **Mickey Shuler**

After finally winning the "Joe Must Go" war, they may be sending the "Turn Bruce Loose" bumper stickers to the printer. Welcome to New Jersey, Bruce Coslet.

It could be a tough year for the one-time Bengal in his first head-coaching assignment. He'll find a chopped-up offensive line, a wide receiver corps in need of new talent, and a defense with plenty of holes. Even a top personnel man like new GM Dick Steinberg will be hard-pressed to fill all of them.

Quarterback doesn't seem to be one of the problem spots. Ken O'Brien (288 for 477, 3,346 yards, 12 TDs) will battle pal Tony Eason, one of many ex-Patriots joining Steinberg in New Jersey. Either choice is a good one — if the offensive line cooperates.

RG Dan Alexander's retirement raises more questions about the front line. Gs Mike Haight and Dave Cadigan have been disappointments, and RT Reggie McElroy may never fully recover from his most recent knee surgery. Tom Rehder and Dave Zawatson will try to fill in. LT Jeff Criswell is decent, and C Jim Sweeney is first-rate. If Trevor Matich can play center, Sweeney goes back to guard, where he also excels.

With vet Wes Walker gone, WR Al Toon (63 for 693) gets new help from No. 2 pick Reggie Rembert. JoJo Townsell (45 for 787) was a pleasant surprise at WR last year. A healthy TE Mickey Shuler (29 for 322 in limited time) would be a major help. He's joined by Keith Neubert (28 for 302).

Improved line-blocking will also help the running game. Top gainer Johnny Hector (177 for 702) and banged-up Freeman McNeil (80 for 352) are fine RBs. FB Roger Vick has shown flashes, and top pick Blair Thomas is a winner.

Youth will be served on the defensive front, where DLE Dennis Byrd, DREs Ron Stallworth and Marvin Washington, and NT Scott Mersereau bear no comparison to the Jets' once-fearsome Sack Exchange. DLE Marty Lyons may have another year left.

If the Jets can decide what to do with '89 No. 1 draftee Jeff Lageman, they'll be in decent shape. Alex Gordon and Kyle Clifton are solid. The Jet secondary is inconsistent. RCB James Hasty is terrific; FS Erik McMillan is even better.

AFC Central
PITTSBURGH STEELERS
1989 Finish: Second (tied)
1990 Prediction: First

Louis Lipps   **Rod Woodson**

Nothing beats winning to raise a team's confidence. As the Steelers won five of their last six to qualify for the '89 play-offs, QB Bubby Brister proclaimed, "We could be the team of the nineties."

Maybe, just maybe. Brister hit on 187 of his 342 passes for 2,365 yards and 9 TDs to lead a balanced, though weak, attack. There's nothing behind Brister, which must keep coach Chuck Noll awake on many fall evenings.

RBs Tim Worley (195 carries for 770 yards) and Merril Hoge (186 for 621) do the heavy ground work for the Steelers. But the team of the nineties will need a better Worley and a Hoge who plays every week like he played in the play-offs. Dwight Stone and Rodney Carter back up.

Though he caught only 50 balls for 944 yards and 5 TDs, WR Louis Lipps is a real Steel City leader. Wideouts Derek Hill and Weegie Thompson should see the ball frequently, with Mike Mularkey (22 for 326), top draft pick Eric Green, and Plan B Billy Griggs at TE.

The offensive line should be in decent shape, especially if LG John Rienstra stays healthy. Starters John Jackson and Tunch Ilkin get support from backup (and future starting) T Tom Ricketts, with Rienstra and Terry Long at G and natural guard Dermontti Dawson at center.

Except for pressuring the passer (major failure), the Steeler defensive line is adequate. Vet DLE Keith Willis needs help from Aaron Jones and A.J. Jenkins, with Tim Johnson a possible choice at NT.

The linebacker crew is in decent enough shape, led by ROLB Greg Lloyd. Bryan Hinkle plays on the opposite side, with David Little and Hardy Nickerson on the inside.

RCB Rod Woodson is the clear-cut leader of the secondary. His three interceptions, four forced fumbles, and three fumble recoveries charged up the defense last season. His cornerback mate, Dwayne Woodruff, gets it done, but CB Delton Hall has occasional problems. FS Thomas Everett always plays tough, and SS Carnell Lake was the '89 season's most pleasant surprise. Woodson is the league's top kickoff-return man.

AFC Central
CINCINNATI BENGALS
1989 Finish: Fourth
1990 Prediction: Second

James Brooks   **Boomer Esiason**

Talk about yo-yos. The Bengals have
gone from 4–11 to the Super Bowl to the AFC
Central cellar in three seasons. Makes it
tough to figure coach Sam Wyche's team.

Although the other three Central teams
went to the postseason play-offs, you can't
figure the Bengals as a last-place team. QB
Boomer Esiason (258 of 455, 3,525 yards, 28
TDs) has been the AFC leader the last two
seasons. Bothered by a sore arm for more
than a year, he seemed to regain the missing zip on his throws toward the end of '89.

If RB Ickey Woods bounces back from
serious knee surgery that cost him 14 games
last season, the Bengal running game will
be in fine shape. Veteran James Brooks (221
for 1,239 yards, a league-leading 5.6 yards
per carry, 7 TDs, 37 catches for 306 yards)

put on a brilliant one-man show. He got little help from former top draftee Eric Ball (98 for 391) and FB Stanford Jennings (83 for 293). Paul Palmer is on hand, too.

Led by Tim McGee (65 catches for 1,211 yards and 8 TDs), the receiver corps is in great shape. Swift Eddie Brown (52 for 814) was a wonderful partner, and TE Rodney Holman (50 for 736) is one of the AFC's best.

There's good news and bad news up front. There's no one better than LT Anthony Munoz, but Pro Bowl RG Max Montoya moved to the Raiders as a Plan B free agent. The line, including LG Bruce Reimers, C Bruce Kuzerski, and RT Joe Walter, was pretty banged up in '89.

When he's healthy, DLE Jim Skow is first-rate, but his size causes problems. NT Tim Krumrie amazed the experts when he recovered from his Super Bowl broken leg. DRE Jason Buck hasn't made it yet.

While LOLB Leon White, LILB Carl Zander, and RILB Joe Kelly should be back at their usual posts, ROLB Reggie Williams has retired, opening the way for Kevin Walker or rookies James Francis and Bernard Clark.

SS David Fulcher (8 interceptions, 107 team-leading tackles) is the leader of a better-than-decent secondary, including corners Lewis Billups and Eric Thomas and FS Rickey Dixon.

One of these days, Wyche will find a placekicker who'll get him a win or two. Jim Breech hasn't been the answer.

AFC Central
HOUSTON OILERS
1989 Finish: Second (tied)
1990 Prediction: Third

Ray Childress   **Warren Moon**

Now that coach Jerry Glanville has been shuffled off to Atlanta, the Oilers won't be leaving tickets for Elvis Presley, the Incredible Hulk, or Mutant Ninja Turtles of any age. They hope, instead, to leave opponents in their wake, with their high-powered run-and-shoot offense and new 4–3 defense.

Though he's age 33 in your program, QB Warren Moon (280 of 464, 3,631 yards, 23 TDs) doesn't play like a 33-year-old. That's good. A run-and-shoot QB must be durable. If he goes down, unhappy Cody Carlson gets the call, if he's still around.

In the new one-back set, Alonzo Highsmith (128 for 531) will probably get the first shot, with Allen Pinkett (94 for 449) getting more time as a receiver. Mike Rozier and

Lorenzo White may be in no-man's-land.

In an offense that eats up receivers, the Oilers have a bunch. Start with vets like Ernest Givins (55 for 794) and Drew Hill (66 for 938, 8 TDs). Then add in returnees like Curtis Duncan, Leonard Harris, Haywood Jeffries, and Plan B newcomers like Gerald McNeil, Bernard Ford, and Carl Harry.

Does anyone have a pair of guards as good as Houston's All-Pro Bruce Matthews and Mike Munchak? C Jay Pennison is excellent, but the Oilers might find a tackle to join Bruce Davis, Dean Steinkuhler, and David Williams.

The switch to the 4-3 means the Oilers need another defensive tackle. Veteran DE Ray Childress could man one tackle spot, possibly joining troubled Doug Smith. Sean Jones, Richard Byrd, and William Fuller are the ends.

The Oiler linebackers are loyal workers, though they excite no one. Look for top pick Lamar Lathon, Robert Lyles, John Grimsley, Al Smith, and Johnny Meads to get plenty of action.

The secondary is in shambles. Houston will score plenty of points. The question is: Can they stop anyone? FS Jeff Donaldson and Tracey Eaton both left as Plan B's, so LCB Steve Brown may move to FS. RCB Patrick Allen and SS Bubba McDowell are back, but real help is needed here.

PK Tony Zendejas and P Greg Montgomery are set. McNeil and other Plan B pickups strengthen the return teams.

AFC Central
CLEVELAND BROWNS
1989 Finish: First
1990 Prediction: Fourth

Michael Dean Perry   **Webster Slaughter**

At the start of every season, the so-called experts write off the Cleveland Browns. At the end — four times in the last five years — the Browns win the AFC Central championship. They shouldn't win in 1990. But they probably will.

As long as QB Bernie Kosar (303 of 513, 3,533 yards, 18 TDs) is healthy, the Browns should move the ball. He doesn't look good when he throws, but he seems to get the ball there. Mike Pagel, who thinks he should be playing more, will likely back up again.

Big RB Kevin Mack, who returned from prison late last season, gives the Browns a fine running attack. He rejoins the man with a thousand moves, RB Eric Metcalf (187 carries for 633 yards, 54 catches for 397 yards, 10 TDs overall), who makes it exciting every time he touches the ball. Top pick Leroy Hoard, Tim Manoa, and Barry Redden provide depth.

The outside receivers, led by Webster Slaughter (65 for 1,236 and TDs of 97, 80, and 77 yards) and Reggie Langhorne (60 for 749), are outstanding. TE is a problem, with Ozzie Newsome (29 for 324) deciding to play another year after planning to retire.

The offensive line could be a disaster, unless guards Ted Banker and Dan Fike are healthy. C Gregg Rakoczy returns after a so-so year, with Mike Baab now on hand to back up. Ts Ricky Bolden and Paul Farren should be set, with youngsters like Tony Jones, Kevin Simons, and Ben Jefferson ready to take over.

DRT Michael Dean Perry (7 sacks) leads the defensive front, with aging Carl Hairston holding off Chris Pike for now. Another ancient, Al Baker (7½ sacks), returns at DLE opposite Robert Banks.

The linebacker corps is first-rate, which thrills defensive-minded head coach Bud Carson. Vet LLB Clay Matthews joins MLB Mike Johnson and RLB Dave Grayson, with Van Waiters ready to step in.

Ex-Patriot CB Ray Clayborn replaces departed Hanford Dixon in the secondary. LCB Frank Minnifield has slipped badly. SS Felix Wright and FS Thane Gash are OK.

PK Matt Bahr and P Bryan Wagner should be back, though a return man must be found to replace Ice Cube McNeil.

AFC West
KANSAS CITY CHIEFS
1989 Finish: Second
1990 Prediction: First

Irv Eatman   **Deron Cherry**

The AFC's best record (5–2–1) over the final half of the '89 season moved the Kaycee Chiefs from fifth to second in the AFC West. The schedule toughens considerably in '90, but the personnel to continue the improvement may be on hand.

The Nigerian Nightmare, RB Christian Okoye (a league-leading 1,480 yards on 370 carries), is the focus of the offense. Though he has been prone to injury, the huge (6–1, 260 pounds) Okoye figures to dominate enemy defenses again. The rest of the running game, including James Saxon and Herman Heard, is fairly ordinary.

QB Steve DeBerg (196 of 324, 2,529 yards, 11 TDs) tries to keep his QB job at age 36, after 13 seasons. One of the game's premier ball-handlers but an inconsistent passer, he'll be hard-pressed to hold off Steve Pelluer and Mike Elkins.

There's nothing wrong with the Chiefs' receiving corps that a superquick outside man wouldn't improve. But ex-Lion Pete Mandley (35 catches for 476 yards) and vet Stephone Paige (44 for 759) will get the job done. TE Jonathan Hayes (18 for 229) is a vastly improved blocker.

The offensive line is loaded with question marks. C Mike Webster is an ancient 38, LG Rich Baldinger is a limited player, and LT John Alt and RG David Lutz have spent lots of time with the team doctor. RT Irv Eatman is adequate. Kaycee signed a bunch of Plan B linemen.

K.C. is loaded at NT, with a healthy Bill Maas and Dan Saleaumua. DLE Neil Smith came up big in his second year, but DRE Leonard Griffin needs some relief.

ROLB Derrick Thomas (10 sacks) made the Pro Bowl as a rookie and shows promise of becoming an NFL superstar. The rest of the group, including LOLB Chris Martin (82 tackles) and inside men Dino Hackett, Walker Lee Ashley, and top pick Percy Snow, is good enough.

The secondary may be the league's best, led by Chief all-timer FS Deron Cherry and a pair of Pro Bowl CBs, Albert Lewis and Kevin Ross. SS Kevin Porter has taken over for longtime vet Lloyd Burruss.

Ex-Giant PK Bjorn Nittmo joins the kicking group that includes P Kelly Goodburn and PK Nick Lowery.

AFC West
DENVER BRONCOS
1989 Finish: First
1990 Prediction: Second

Bobby Humphrey   **Dennis Smith**

The next time the Broncos earn a Super
Bowl trip, they should "just say no." Coach
Dan Reeves's team has suffered through
three straight embarrassments, the final
blow coming in a 55–10 bombing by the
49ers last January.

On the plus side, the Broncos seem to
bounce back to beat everyone in the AFC.
Why not? Reeves is a brilliant coach, Elway
is a tremendous leader, the Denver defense
seems to be improving, and no one has
figured a way to win in Denver.

Elway (223 of 416 for 3,051 yards and 18
TDs) remains ever-dangerous. With the
possible exceptions of Dan Marino and Joe
Montana, whom would you prefer to see
with the ball when you need a last-second
score? Gary Kubiak is a solid backup.

If RB Bobby Humphrey (294 for 1,151 yards and 7 TDs) is as good as his rookie year seems to indicate, the Broncos, at last, have a running game. FB Melvin Bratton looks like a future star, too.

Up front, the tackles remain a major problem. LT Gerald Perry appears lazy and out of shape; RT Ken Lanier is slipping. There's decent depth elsewhere, with vet Keith Bishop available behind G Jim Juriga and young Doug Widell and C Keith Kartz.

No one picked up Plan B free agent TE Clarence Kay, who should team with Orson Mobley and newcomer David Little. WR Vance Johnson (76 catches for 1,095 yards, 7 TDs) is the receiver of choice, backed up by Mark Jackson (28 for 446) and a healthy Ricky Nattiel (10 for 183).

The Broncs picked up Plan B DE Robb White and Mark Mraz to bolster aging Alphonso Carreker and younger Ron Holmes and Warren Powers. All-Pro RILB Karl Mecklenburg may be at the top of his game but needs more help than Rick Dennison offered last year. OLBs Michael Brooks and Simon Fletcher have strengthened the Denver D.

SS Dennis Smith, a three-time Pro Bowler, is the leader of an overachieving secondary. LCB Tyrone Braxton merits an edge over RCB Wymon Henderson, though neither appears to be Reeves's idea of a perfect cornerback. No. 1 draft pick FS Steve Atwater won a starting role early in his rookie season. He should be around awhile.

AFC West
LOS ANGELES RAIDERS
1989 Finish: Third
1990 Prediction: Third

Mervyn Fernandez　　　　　　　　**Howie Long**

If, as they say, the Raiders have gone Hollywood, the reviews are, at best, mixed. Al Davis has plenty of talented players, but whether there are enough at enough positions remains to be seen.

The QB picture remains cloudy. The battle between Steve Beuerlein (108 of 217, 1,677 yards, 13 TDs) and Jay Schroeder (91 of 194, 1,550 yards, 8 TDs) continues. Both are big and strong, and can throw long, a requirement for Raider QBs. Neither is headed for the Hall of Fame.

There's a ton of depth in the running game, with comebacker Marcus Allen (69 for 293), Vance Mueller (48 for 161), Steve Strachan, Kerry Porter, and — depending upon the Kansas City Royals' fortunes — leading gainer Bo Jackson (173 for 950).

A healthy Tim Brown will brighten an already-solid receiving picture, led by ex-Bear Willie Gault (28 for 690) and Mervyn Fernandez (57 for 1,069 yards, 9 TDs). Mike Dyal is a first-rate TE.

The addition of ex-Bengal Pro Bowl G Max Montoya bolsters a decent offensive line, long the key to Raider success. Steve Wisniewski should join Montoya in the starting lineup, with depth from '89 starter John Gesek. A somewhat shaky Rory Graves rejoins Steve Wright and Bruce Wilkerson at the tackles, with vet Don Mosebar at center.

If DE Howie Long is healthy, the defensive line will be in fairly good shape. Questionable top pick Anthony Smith, Greg Townsend, Scott Davis, and Mike Wise provide depth at the ends, with aging Bob Golic and Bill Pickel splitting time at NT.

Linebacking is a Raider concern. For the second straight year, the Silver and Black loaded up with Plan B LB talent, includng Ron Burton, Bruce Klostermann, and Joe Campbell on the '90 list, plus No. 2 pick Aaron Wallace. Last year's Plan B addition, Tom Benson, rejoins OLB Emanuel King, with 33-year-old Jerry Robinson in the middle.

CBs Terry McDaniel and Lionel Washington are adequate, with McDaniel rating slightly higher. The return of Vann McElroy will bolster the last line of defense, which features Mike Harden and Eddie Anderson.

AFC West
SAN DIEGO CHARGERS
1989 Finish: Fifth
1990 Prediction: Fourth

Leslie O'Neal   Billy Joe Tolliver

If it makes anyone feel better, the Chargers were the NFL's best fifth-place team in 1989. With new GM Bobby Beathard now in place, some solid coaching staff improvements, and a full season for strong-armed QB Billy Joe Tolliver, San Diego is going in the right direction.

Tolliver (89 of 185, 1,097 yards, 5 TDs) took over for the final four games in '89 and earned a solid chance to take over in '90. Expensive ex-Bear Jim McMahon (176 of 318, 2,132 yards, 10 TDs) was released, so there's plenty of pressure on Tolliver.

When RB Gary Anderson (off to Tampa) held out for the entire '89 season, he dealt the Chargers a deadly blow. But San Diego discovered Marion Butts (170 carries for 683 yards) and Tim Spencer (134 for 521).

WR Anthony Miller (75 catches for 1,252 yards), the Charger '89 MVP, heads a young but talented receiver group. Jamie Holland, Quinn Early, and Wayne Walker should split time on the other side. If Early and TE Rod Bernstine are healthy, the Chargers will be, too.

A revamped offensive line still needs more revamping. C Courtney Hall was a pleasant surprise as a rookie last year, but the rest of the group, like Ts Joel Patten and Brett Miller and Gs David Richards and Broderick Thompson, need help. If Dennis McKnight and Larry Williams return healthy and Plan B free agents Michael Simmonds and Tom Toth can play, help will be on its way.

Pro Bowl DLE Lee Williams (AFC-leading 14 sacks) leads the defensive front, along with superrookie DRE Burt Grossman (10 sacks) and NT Joe Phillips.

OLBs Leslie O'Neal (12½ sacks) and Billy Ray Smith are outstanding. ILBs Gary Plummer and Cedric Figaro don't match up. Watch top pick Junior Seau shine.

LCB Gill Byrd keyed an improved Charger secondary that had 23 interceptions, most in San Diego in 28 seasons. Ex-Raider Sam Seale improved on the opposite corner but still has a way to go. FS Vencie Glenn is a big-play defender. SS Martin Bayless might be hard-pressed to retain his spot. Changes will be made in the kicking game. PK John Carney and P John Kidd are on hand as free agents.

AFC West
SEATTLE SEAHAWKS
1989 Finish: Fourth
1990 Prediction: Fifth

Joe Nash   Brian Blades

After years of challenging for the AFC
West title, the Seahawks seemed lucky to
finish 7–9 in '89. It may not get better in '90.

The famous Ground Chuck (for coach
Chuck Knox) almost ground to a halt. And
the passing game was hurt by QB Dave
Kreig's in-and-out play and too-many
fumbles.

Kreig (286 of 499, 3,309 yards, 21 TDs) was
at his best as Seattle took three of its last
four. But his 18 fumbles and 20 interceptions had to bother Seattle fans. For Kelly
Stouffer, the QB of the future, the future may
be now.

The leader of Ground Chuck, RB Curt
Warner (194 carries for 631 yards), is gone,
off to the L.A. Rams as a Plan B free agent.
John L. Williams (146 for 499 plus 76 catches

for 657 yards) should return at FB, but there's plenty of work ahead. Seattle got only 3.4 yards per running play in '89.

Steve Largent, football's all-time receiving leader, has retired, but WR Brian Blades (77 catches for 1,063 yards) is a talent. Paul Skansi (39 for 488) or a healthy Tommy Kane could start on the opposite side. Watch for young TE Travis McNeal, who showed some spark as a rookie.

Up front, LT Andy Heck was a starter by the end of his rookie year. He'll join RT Mike Wilson, who's 35, or Ron Mattes, with Edwin Bailey and Bryan Millard at the guards, and Grant Feasel or Joe Toffelmire at center.

Top pick DT Cortez Kennedy bolsters the front line. DE Rufus Porter, who usually plays on passing downs only, led in sacks with 10½ and forced fumbles. NT Joe Nash (8 sacks, 92 tackles) has gone from extra man to No. 1 man in only a couple of seasons. DE Jacob Green has seen better days, and DE Jeff Bryant isn't doing it.

With Brian Bosworth probably done, Seattle is pleased with the play of ILB Darren Comeaux, who joins David Wyman. Neither has enough size. Tony Woods and M.L. Johnson must improve on the outside.

Patrick Hunter and Dwayne Harper seem to have settled in at the corners, though they lack size. SS Nesby Glasgow returns from an outstanding year, with too-slow Eugene Robinson back at FS.

P Ruben Rodriguez may give way to Rick Donnelly, with Norm Johnson the PK.

Detroit's version of the run-and-shoot offense
is perfectly suited to the style of 1989 Rookie
of the Year Barry Sanders.

National
Football
Conference
Team Previews

NFC East
NEW YORK GIANTS
1989 Finish: First
1990 Prediction: First

Dave Meggett   **Carl Banks**

With just a few aging players and no enormous holes to fill, the Giants begin the nineties with enough talent to hold off the hard-charging Eagles and Redskins.

Gutsy Phil Simms (228 of 405, 3,061 yards, 14 TDs) starts his 12th year as the Giant QB, ready to enter the top-20 list of all-time NFL passers. Jeff Hostetler, who went 2–0 as a starter in '89, is the backup.

The running game should be interesting. Joe Morris may be done after a broken foot cost him the entire '89 season. Seemingly ageless O.J. Anderson (325 carries for 1,023 yards, 14 TDs), last year's surprising hero, is back. Both Morris and Anderson were available on Plan B lists. Mo Carthon remains a rock-solid blocking back, while youngsters like top pick Rodney

Hampton, Lewis Tillman, and Pro Bowl return specialist Dave Meggett offer exciting possibilities.

The receivers are sound, even if they don't scare anyone. Odessa Turner (38 for 467, 4 TDs), Lionel Manuel (33 for 539), and Mark Ingram are dependable. If former All-Pro TE Mark Bavaro isn't back from knee surgery, the Giants will rely on Howard Cross and ex-Oiler Bob Mrosko, good-block, no-catch types.

The offensive line is in wonderful shape, with fine youngsters like Jumbo Elliott and Doug Riesenberg at tackle and Eric Moore and William Roberts at guard. Vet Bart Oates returns at center, with Brian Williams ready to step in soon.

Pro Bowl DRE Leonard Marshall (9½ sacks) is the best pass-rusher up front, where DLE Eric Dorsey is superb against the run. NT Erik Howard is coming fast, joined by No. 2 pick Mike Fox.

In his 10th year, All-Pro OLB Lawrence Taylor (15 sacks despite a broken ankle) remains the game's best. OLB Carl Banks (97 tackles) is just a hair behind. ILBs Gary Reasons and Pepper Johnson aren't in their class.

Look for '89 surprise Myron Guyton to move to FS, with Greg Jackson getting a full shot at SS. CB Mark Collins is one of the NFL's best.

If PK Raul Allegre stays healthy, the kicking game (with P Sean Landeta) is in great shape.

NFC East
PHILADELPHIA EAGLES
1989 Finish: Second
1990 Prediction: Second

Randall Cunningham   **Clyde Simmons**

With the 1989 NFC East title firmly in their mitts, the Eagles dropped the ball in Game 15 in New Orleans. Finishing second, they were blown out of the play-offs by the L.A. Rams. What began as a brilliant season wound up in ashes.

The coming season should be better. The Eagles have the NFL's most exciting quarterback, one of the finest defensive lines, the game's No. 1 tight end, and an outstanding cornerback. They might be a little short on depth, and there's no superstar running back; but there's enough talent to make a dent in the Super Bowl tournament.

Start with QB Randall Cunningham. He hit 290 of his 532 pass attempts for 3,400 yards and 21 TDs. He also led the club in rushing with 104 carries for 621 yards. More importantly, he seems to have the key to beating the NFC East rival Giants.

The RBs aren't much. Keith Byars (133 carries for 452 yards) will never be a great one, but he's OK. His running mate Anthony Toney (172 for 582) gets it done. A healthy TE Keith Jackson (63 catches for 648) is a key. When he's in there, the Birds are tough to beat. If WR Mike Quick comes back from a pair of knee operations, so much the better. There isn't enough speed on the outside, where Ron Johnson and Cris Carter should return.

RG Ron Solt, a former All-Pro who has slipped, is still the best of the line, which includes Ts Matt Darwin and Ron Heller, G Mike Schad, and C David Alexander.

The awesome defensive front is led by All-Pro DLE Reggie White (11 sacks). The Minister of Defense makes stars of DRE Clyde Simmons (15½ sacks) and DRT Jerome Brown (10½ sacks). DLT Mike Pitts completes the group.

Linebacking is in good shape, with Seth Joyner and Al Harris surrounding MLB Byron Evans. Jessie Small is a comer here.

All-Pro CB Eric Allen (eight interceptions) and top pick Ben Smith head the secondary, which lacks depth and speed. Izel Jenkins may return at one corner, with Andre Waters and veteran Wes Hopkins at safety.

Who does the kicking for the Eagles? Which week is it? Flub one kick and coach Buddy Ryan gets on the phone.

NFC East
WASHINGTON REDSKINS
1989 Finish: Third
1990 Prediction: Third

Art Monk   **Darryl Grant**

The Washington Redskins wish the '90 season had started months ago. Winning their final five 1989 games, using young talent in place of injured veterans, and signing some quality Plan B free agents, the 'Skins are ready to start the new decade.

With Doug Williams gone, Mark Rypien (280 of 476, 3,768 yards, 22 TDs) has the QB job all to himself. There's good backup help with strong-armed Stan Humphries and capable ex-Giant Jeff Rutledge.

Ex-Tampa Bay star James Wilder may provide needed depth behind premier rusher Gerald Riggs (201 carries for 834 yards). Earnest Byner (134 for 580, 7 TDs) can still get it done despite a decided lack of speed. Jamie Morris left for New England.

There's plenty of talent on the wings, led

by 32-year-old Art Monk (86 catches for 1,186 yards and 8 TDs), Ricky Sanders (80 for 1,138), and Gary Clark (79 for 1,229). No one else in the league owns a more productive trio. TE Jimmie Johnson should make a major impact in '90, taking over from vets Don Warren and Mike Tice.

If RT Joe Jacoby and RG Mark May, both in the over-30 group, can't make it back from '89 injuries, coach Joe Gibbs will begin a major overhaul. Look for Plan B ex-Chief G Mark Adickes to battle with Mark Schlereth and Raleigh McKenzie for a starting role. All-Pro LT Jim Lachey anchors the line, which also features comeback C Jeff Bostic and RT Ed Simmons.

The 'Skins were thrilled with DRE Fred Stokes and DLT Tracy Rocker, who were forced into action last year. They'll join DRT Darryl Grant and DLE Charles Mann (team-leading 9½ sacks), as ex-Saint James Geathers gets healthy.

Plan B ex-Jet Kevin McArthur will seek a starting LB role with disappointing Wilber Marshall, questionable Greg Manusky, and Ravin Caldwell.

Ex-Viking FS Brad Edwards will challenge Todd Bowles (130 tackles) for a full-time job. SS Clarence Vaughn and Alvin Walton (team-leading 137 tackles) should hold their own. But CBs Martin Mayhew, A.J. Johnson, and a healthy Barry Wilburn will have to improve.

The kicking game (P Ralf Mojsiejenko; PK Chip Lohmiller) is in good shape.

NFC East
DALLAS COWBOYS
1989 Finish: Fifth
1990 Prediction: Fourth

Jim Jeffcoat   **Nate Newton**

No doubt about it. Troy Aikman, who still hasn't won an NFL game (he missed the Cowboys' lone victory last year), is the Dallas QB of the future. How far in the future remains to be seen.

Surrounded by little talent, Aikman hit 155 of 293 for 1,749 yards and 9 TDs in his freshman year. He will get better. Meanwhile, fellow freshman Steve Walsh filled in when Aikman was hurt and hit 110 of 219 for 1,371 yards and 5 TDs. He'll be traded.

FB Daryl Johnston (67 carries for 212 yards) is the leading returning rusher. He will start, probably joining top pick Emmitt Smith. If former Redskin Timmy Smith can ever play as he did in Super Bowl XXII, he'll thrill all Texas.

The top returning receivers, Kelvin Martin (46 catches for 644 yards, 2 TDs) and Michael Irvin (26 for 278, 2TDs) are both coming back from serious knee surgery. If healthy, they'll start and play. If not, look to ex-Bear Plan B arrival Dennis McKinnon to do the heavy work. Plan B ex-Card TE Jay Novacek should start for Dallas.

Another Plan B, Tony Slaton, joins an improving offensive line that really needs a solid RT to join LT Mark Tuinei. The guards, veterans Nate Newton and Crawford Ker, are pretty decent. Young Mark Stepnoski could be the 'Pokes' center for a while.

Most teams would be delighted to have DE Jim Jeffcoat, whose 12 sacks kept Cowboy opponents honest during the '89 dog days. Plan B DEs Lybrant Robinson and Anthony Spears might help, as will a strengthened Tony Tolbert. DRT Danny Noonan still hasn't reached his potential, and T Dean Hamel and Willie Broughton aren't strong on pressure.

MLB Eugene Lockhart, the NFL's first defender with more than 200 tackles in a season, leads the linebacker crew. Jesse Solomon is solid, while Ken Norton and Jack Del Rio are fine against the run, weak against the pass.

In-and-out Robert Williams will start at one corner, with Ron Francis and Ike Holt battling at the other. Safeties Vince Albritton and Ray Horton simply lack speed.

Luis Zendejas's run as Cowboy PK will likely be limited; P Mike Saxon should last.

PHOENIX CARDINALS
1989 Finish: Fourth
1990 Prediction: Fifth

Timm Rosenbach   **Tim McDonald**

Thank goodness for the Dallas Cowboys. Only Dallas's 1–15 record kept the sorry Phoenix Cardinals out of the NFC East basement a year ago. Truth is, the Cards could use the schedule break a last-place finish provides.

New Card coach Joe Bugel, fresh off years of success as Redskin boss Joe Gibbs's key assistant, faces enormous problems in his first year in the desert. Phoenix is shaky at QB, though '89 top choice Timm Rosenbach may make it eventually. He'll battle Tom Tupa and '89 starter Gary Hogeboom for the job. There's no solid choice.

Running back is even shakier, though top pick Anthony Thompson helps. Off-season reports indicated that Stump Mitchell (43 carries for 165 yards) was healing nicely after serious knee surgery. Even so, Mitchell has crossed the age-30 barrier and it's unlikely that the old, hard-driving Mitchell will reappear. Age is also taking a toll on top ground-gainer Earl Ferrell (149 for 502), who is reliable though not much more.

Another pair of ancients heads the Cardinal receiver corps: J.T. Smith (62 catches for 778 yards) is 34; Roy Green (44 for 703) is 33. When they're healthy, they're still good. But which hit will be the last? Ernie Jones (45 for 838) will see lots of action.

RG Lance Smith was the most consistent offensive lineman last year, when tackles Luis Sharpe and Tootie Robbins missed nine games between them. C Derek Kennard missed a couple, too. That gave unexpected experience to versatile Joe Wolf and G Mike Zandofsky.

The defensive front isn't in bad shape, if DE David Galloway is healthy and DT Bob Clasby recovers from knee surgery. DE Freddie Joe Nunn missed a month for substance abuse.

The linebackers are the heart of the defense, with Anthony Bell (115 tackles) and Ken Harvey (career-highs in tackles and sacks) on the outside and Eric Hill (91 tackles) in the middle.

Pro Bowl SS Tim McDonald heads the secondary, along with FS Lonnie Young. CBs Carl Carter and Cedric Mack aren't quite as strong.

Pro Bowl P Rich Camarillo is the special-teams star. PK Al Del Greco is shaky.

NFC Central
GREEN BAY PACKERS
1989 Finish: Second
1990 Prediction: First

Don Majkowski   Brian Noble

If the 1990 double wild-card policy had
been in effect in 1989, the Pack would have
been back — in the play-offs. They could
do it this season.

The picture is somewhat cloudy, however. Green Bay won more than its share
of close games, playing a fairly easy
schedule. QB Don Majkowski (353 of 599,
4,318 yards, 27 TDs) appears to be the man
Green Bay has searched for since Hall-of-
Famer Bart Starr retired a couple of decades
ago. Majkowski's tough, he's strong, he's
accurate, he's good. A second straight solid
year will convince doubters. Backup
Anthony Dilweg is still years away.

Majik's (and All-Pro voters') favorite
receiver is the NFL's catch leader, Sterling
Sharpe (90 for 1,423, 12 TDs). Jeff Query (23

for 250) could be excellent on the opposite side. TE Ed West (22 for 269) isn't bad. Backup help is needed, and the Pack signed three Plan B's at these positions.

RB Brent Fullwood (204 carries for 821 yards in '89) was a pleasant surprise, pairing with Keith Woodside (46 for 273, 59 catches for 527 yards). There's depth with Vince Workman, Michael Haddix, and No. 2 pick Darrell Thompson.

Up front, heralded, superstrong T Tony Mandarich must start doing the things people expect him to do. C Blair Bush retired, but Ts Ken Ruettgers and Alan Veingrad and Gs Rich Moran and Ron Hallstrom are solid enough.

Holding the defensive line together may take a miracle. Having All-Pro OLB Tim Harris (19½ sacks) around helps, as Harris often slots as a DE. A healthy Shawn Patterson would be a plus. Blaise Winter and Robert Brown will be there, with Bob Nelson in the middle.

If top pick Tony Bennett can replace retired LOLB John Anderson, the Pack will be in decent shape. Brian Noble and Johnny Holland should return inside, though Green Bay picked up three Plan B free agents.

The secondary is aging, led by 37-year-old RCB Dave Brown. LCB Mark Lee and SS Mark Murphy are both 32. If he stays healthy, Chuck Cecil should replace departed Ken Stills.

Rookie PK Chris Jacke (22–28 FGs, including five game-winners) is first-rate.

NFC Central
DETROIT LIONS
1989 Finish: Third
1990 Prediction: Second

Rodney Peete   **Jerry Ball**

Until last fall, the Detroit Lions hadn't won
five games in a row since 1970. Unfortu-
nately Detroit was 2–9 when the streak
began. Hopefully the season-ending tear
will continue into 1990.

It won't, unless coach Wayne Fontes finds
a pass-rusher, a wide receiver or two, and
a cornerback. Detroit's Silver Stretch offense
spreads the defense, which made last year's
sensational rookie RB, Barry Sanders (280
rushes for 1,470 yards, a 5.3 average, 14
TDs), even better. There's no depth behind
him.

Quarterbacking should be better, with
top pick Andre Ware on hand. Bob Gagli-
ano (117 of 232, 1,671 yards, 6 TDs) ran the
offense during the '89 winning streak. But
Rodney Peete (103 of 1,955, 1,479, 5 TDs)

could be the QB of choice, if he stays healthy — a problem in the stretch offense. The Lions may be ready to give up on Chuck Long.

With four wideouts required in the stretch, the Lions need plenty of help behind Richard Johnson (70 for 1,091 yards, 8 TDs). Walter Stanley, the NFL's top punt-returner, left for Washington via Plan B. Disappointing '89 draft pick John Ford could contribute in '90.

The line can do the job, led by C Kevin Glover, T Lomas Brown, and G Eric Andol-sek. It will get better if Harvey Salem and Mike Utley, both of whom can go at guard and tackle, are ready.

NT Jerry Ball, a 6-1, 300-pounder who had nine sacks, is one of the NFL's very best. DLE Eric Williams works well with Ball, with Kevin Brooks or Keith Ferguson on the opposite side. High draftees Dan Owens and Mark Spindler help. The linebacking corps, led by Pro Bowler LILB Chris Spiel-man and LOLB Jimmy Williams, is the heart of the defense. Michael Cofer and Dennis Gibson play the right side.

LCB Terry Taylor and FS William White are the keys to the secondary, with plenty of Plan B help on the way. If SS Bennie Blades continues to improve, this unit could be solid.

Special teams are another Detroit strength. Reliable PK Eddie Murray made 20 of 21 field-goal attempts, and P Jim Arnold kept opponents backed up.

NFC Central
MINNESOTA VIKINGS
1989 Finish: First
1990 Prediction: Third

Wade Wilson   **Herschel Walker**

You figure out the Vikings. They own, perhaps, the NFL's best overall talent. At the ballpark, however, it never seems to come together. The 41–13 play-off loss to the Niners (OK, the Broncos fared even worse) was a perfect ending to an imperfect season.

Will Herschel Walker (169 carries for 669 yards) become the superstar Minnesota paid so heavily for? Not unless coach Jerry Burns has figured out a better way to get the talented Walker into the Vike offense. Running mates Rick Fenney (151 for 588) and D.J. Dozier (46 for 207) provide more than enough depth.

QB Wade Wilson (194 for 362, 2,543 yards, only 9 TDs) was good enough to go to the Pro Bowl, not good enough to win every week. With Tommy Kramer gone, Rich Gannon may see more action if Wilson remains inconsistent.

WR Anthony (A.C.) Carter (65 for 1,066, 4 TDs) scares every opponent, and Hassan Jones (42 for 694) is solid, but simply not fast enough. TE Steve Jordan (35 for 506) requires some backup help.

Walker's type of running requires big, powerful drive-blockers, not the trap-blocking types who toil in Minny. Adding Plan B Craig Wolfley helps, but RT Tim Irwin is beginning to show his years. The left side is in good shape, with T Gary Zimmerman and G Randall McDaniel. Irwin joins G Todd Kalis and David Huffman on the right. Kirk Lowdermilk returns at C.

The starting defensive line remains one of the NFL's best. All-Pro DRE Chris Doleman had 21 sacks but probably wasn't as effective as All-Pro DRT Keith Millard (18 sacks, despite a separated shoulder). DE Al Noga and DT Henry Thomas are fine on the right, though more depth is needed.

The age of MLB Scott Studwell (36) could be a problem soon. Mike Merriweather and Ray Berry are fine on the outside, with depth again a headache.

SS Joey Browner is among the game's best, and CBs Carl Lee and Reggie Rutland are an outstanding pair. FS Ken Still could solve the weakest link in the secondary, though it would be worse if the other three weren't so good.

NFC Central
CHICAGO BEARS
1989 Finish: Fourth
1990 Prediction: Fourth

Neal Anderson   Steve McMichael

The fourth-place Chicago Bears? Sounds strange, doesn't it? But the Monsters of the Midway played more like pussycats last season. A repeat performance could end Mike Ditka's stormy Bear coaching career.

The Mike Tomczak-Jim Harbaugh QB battle continues. The 6–3, 204-pound Harbaugh (111 for 178, 1,204 yards, 5 TDs) gets the edge if he can learn to hang in the pocket a little longer. Tomczak (156 of 306, 2,058 yards, 16TDs) is a limited player.

Blessed with a rich, new contract, RB Neal Anderson, the Bears' top rusher (1,275 yards), catcher (50 receptions), and TD scorer (15), remains the biggest offensive weapon. FB Brad Muster (327 yards) must bounce back from back surgery.

There's little speed at the WR spots,

where Wendell Davis (26 catches for 397 yards) and Ron Morris (30 for 486) should be the starters, backed up by former starter Dennis Gentry. Jim Thornton (24 for 392) rates the starting nod at TE, though Cap Boso (17 for 182) will get plenty of action.

Up front, age is catching up with tackles Keith Van Horne and Jim Covert, who has gone backward because of frequent injuries. Gs Tom Thayer and Mark Bortz are steady, and C Jay Hilgenberg is simply the best. Plan B T Kurt Becker may help.

The defensive line, long a Bear feature, could become a problem. RT Dan Hampton, now 33, comes off double-knee surgery. The Bears went 2–10 after he went down last year. RE Richard Dent, a frequent All-Pro, has slipped a couple of notches, and '89 rookie LE Trace Armstrong has a way to go. LT Steve McMichael is solid.

Superstar MLB Mike Singletary (151 team-leading tackles) anchors the defensive unit, surrounded by Ron Rivera (96 tackles) and John Roper. Former starter Jim Morrissey could return after a kidney injury.

CBs Donnell Woolford and Vestee Jackson struggled last season, Woolford because he was a rookie, Jackson because the pass-rush died. Dave Duerson and Shaun Gayle may return at safety, though Markus Paul and top pick Mark Carrier could push them.

Kevin Butler is a fine PK. P Maury Buford will try to hold off Kent Sullivan.

NFC Central
TAMPA BAY BUCCANEERS
1989 Finish: Fifth
1990 Prediction: Fifth

Mark Carrier   **Harry Hamilton**

On paper, the Tampa Bay Bucs are not a fifth-place team. On the field, they are, and that's what counts in the NFL. Coach Ray Perkins's squad is making progress, slow progress. Patience, Tampa, patience.

QB Vinny Testaverde now looks like a winner who'll get even better when the Bucs get a running game. Still his 258 for 480 performance (22 interceptions) for 3,133 yards and 20 TDs wasn't bad. If anything happens to Vinny, there's no one else.

As mentioned, the Bucs need No. 2 pick RB Reggie Cobb to stay out of trouble. The '89 group, led by Lars Tate (589 yards, but 167 carries, only 3.5 yards per carry) and FB William Howard (108 for 357, only 3.3), work hard, but that's about it.

Testaverde is blessed with a couple of

decent receivers. Mark Carrier (86 for 1,422 yards, 9 TDs) had the best season ever for a Buc WR. He needs a partner with speed on the other side. TE Ron Hall (30 for 331) is solid, but there's no depth.

Perkins's offensive line is about 60% complete. Everyone likes LT Paul Gruber and C Randy Grimes. Young RG John Bruhin is a potential star. But that's where it ends. T Rob Taylor and G Tom McHale and Mark Cooper are back; G Mike Simmonds left (Plan B) for San Diego.

DLE Reuben Davis is the lone star on the defensive front line. The Bucs will hang on with DE Robert Goff and NT Curt Jarvis until help arrives.

The linebacking corps is the pride of the defense. The key is the development of top '90 pick Keith McCants and '89 top draftee OLB Broderick Thomas, who can be a fine pass-rusher. Winston Moss and Kevin Murphy (team-leading 6 sacks) work the outside, too, with Ervin Randle the leader inside.

Overall, the secondary is fair, though both safeties, FS Harry Hamilton (6 interceptions) and SS Mark Robinson (6 interceptions, three forced fumbles, three recovered fumbles), are pretty decent. LCB Ricky Reynolds is adequate; RCB Rod Jones isn't. Plan B Eric Everett and Rodney Rice will challenge at the corners.

PK Donald Igwebuike is automatic from 40 yards in, though his kickoffs aren't much. P Chris Mohr must continue to improve.

NFC West
SAN FRANCISCO 49ERS
1989 Finish: First
1990 Prediction: First

Harris Barton   **Roger Craig**

Can the team of the eighties become the team of the nineties? Why not? The 49ers, off two straight Super Bowl victories, return with all of the talent that blew Denver away in Supe XXIV. They're joined by a bunch of "name" players off the Plan B list. (San Francisco lost only one free agent.)

At age 34, QB Joe (The Best Ever?) Montana could well repeat his '89 season (271 of 386, 3,521 yards, 26 TDs). That would keep Steve Young (64 of 92, 1,001 yards, 8 TDs) on the bench, unless he gets his wish for a trade.

Any Niner QB benefits from a corps of superreceivers, led by the NFL's best, Jerry Rice (82 catches for 1,483 yards and 17 TDs). With almost any other club, John Taylor (60 for 1,077, plus 36 punt returns for 417 yards) would be the No. 1 guy. Watch out if Mike Sherrard finally gets healthy. Brent Jones (40 for 500) and Wesley Walls should be back at TE.

High-stepping Roger Craig (271 carries for 1,054 yards, 49 catches for 473 yards) and Tom Rathman (79 for 305, 73 catches for 616 yards) lead a superb cast of running backs. Top pick little Dexter Carter should excite.

The front five (Ts Bubba Paris and Harris Barton, Gs Guy McIntyre and Bruce Collie, and C Jesse Sapolu) is outstanding, though coach George Seifert would like a little more depth. Plan B pickup C Wayne Radloff could find a spot.

Without a flashy superstar, the defensive front is probably somewhat underrated. But ends Pierce Holt, Larry Roberts, and Kevin Fagan are solid, and Michael Carter and Pete Kugler get it done. Ex-Bill Fred Smerlas should help.

OLBs Charles Haley and Keena Turner are still solid citizens, though a young backup for Turner may be in order. Ex-Raider Matt Millen and Michael Walter should hold up the middle.

The secondary features hard-hitting (too hard?) Ronnie Lott at FS, joined by Chet Brooks (replacing Jeff Fuller). The corners are fine, with Darryl Pollard, Don Griffin, and newcomer Eric Davis.

Like the rest of the club, special teams are sound, though on this nearly perfect club, there are questions about P Barry Helton and PK Mike Cofer.

NFC West
LOS ANGELES RAMS
1989 Finish: Second
1990 Prediction: Second

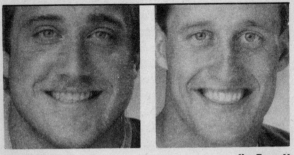

Kevin Greene   Jim Everett

Talk about being in the wrong place at the wrong time. That's the L.A. Rams. While the 49ers have won four Super Bowls on the way to becoming the team of the eighties, the Rams have been the regular runners-up in the NFC West.

Despite losing some serious talent in the Plan B dealings, the Rams still have the best chance of unseating the champion Niners. QB Jim Everett deserved a Pro Bowl shot after a 304 for 518 performance that produced 4,310 yards and 29 TDs in '89. (Only Green Bay's Don Majkowski had more yards, 4,318.) Problem: Everett's technique tends to break down at times. Mark Herrmann is a professional backup.

There's plenty of backfield talent, especially with the arrival of Seattle Plan B Curt

Warner. Greg Bell (272 for 1,137, 15 TDs) may lose his job. For depth, look to folks like Cleveland Gary and Robert Delpino, solid citizens both.

The Rams are blessed with great receivers, though you never really have enough. Henry Ellard (70 for 1,382, 8 TDs) is among the very best, and the Giants will never forget Flipper Anderson (44 for 1,146, 26 yards per catch), who beat them in the playoffs. Pete Holohan is a fine TE.

Up front, age is the problem. RT Jackie Slater is 36; C Doug Smith, 33; and LT Irv Pankey, 32. All-Pro Tom Newberry should join G Joe Milinichik, replacing Tony Slaton (Plan B). Top pick Bern Brostek is the future C.

The Rams' defensive front is improving, though there's room for more. Mike Piel should be back at DRT with Doug Reed and Bill Hawkins on the left. Alvin Wright is the NT.

LOLB Kevin Greene (16½ sacks) leads the 'backers. A healthy ILB Fred Strickland would make Greene even better. Mike Wilcher still has some football left, joining Larry Kelm and Mel Owens.

With longtime Ram LeRoy Irvin released and LCB Jerry Gray slated to move to SS, there could be some problems in the secondary. Darryl Henley might be one corner, with Michael Stewart and Anthony Newman slated for major playing time. Ex-Jet Bobby Humphrey and No. 2 pick Pat Terrell figure, too.

NFC West
ATLANTA FALCONS
1989 Finish: Fourth
1990 Prediction: Third

Chris Miller   **John Settle**

And Jerry Glanville thought he had problems in Houston. The new Falcon coach has a massive job ahead in Atlanta, though the first steps have been good ones.

QB Chris Miller is one, off a 280 for 526 performance in '89 that produced 3,459 yards and 16 TDs. At 6–2 and 200 pounds, Miller is mobile enough to run Glanville's quick red-gun offense. Having Miller allowed Atlanta to deal the top draft pick (Jeff George).

Low-slung RB John Settle (he's 5–9, 210 pounds) is the Falcons' most effective ball-carrier (179 carries for 689 yards). He may rejoin Keith Jones (52 for 202) for another go-round, though neither is a championship-type back. Glanville will shop.

Both Michael Haynes (off a poor 40 catches for 681 yards) and Shawn Collins

(58 for 862) will play major roles this season, though ex-Colt Andre Rison is the new "main man." If Atlanta goes to a run-and-shoot offense, Floyd Dixon or George Thomas will also get the call. If not, Atlanta needs a tight end — badly.

The Falcon offensive line is a mixed bag. RG Bill Fralic is one of the NFL's best; so is ex-Colt Chris Hinton. LT Mike Kenn was, but has slipped. RT Houston Hoover is better at guard. Jamie Dukes should be back at center. Plan B arrivals like Ronnie Lee, Mike Ruether, and Ben Utt could help.

The defensive front could be a problem, too. NT Tony Casillas is unhappy in Atlanta and could be dealt. DRE Rick Bryan might be done (neck nerve injury), which will return Ben Thomas to the lineup. DLE Mike Gann led the Falcons with 27 QB hurries.

The LBs could be Glanville's biggest asset. LOLB Aundray Bruce is plenty tough; so is RILB Jessie Tuggle (team tackle leader with 183). LILB John Rade and injury-prone Marcus Cotton will rejoin ROLB Tim Green, who might be better as a DE.

Unless RCB Neon Deion Sanders decides to play baseball full-time, the Falcons are set at one spot. He's the NFL's best return man, too. LCB Bobby Butler can still get it done. Tim Gordon and Brian Jordan are the returning safeties, with vet CB Scott Case possibly moving there.

Scott Fulhage should handle the punting, with Greg Davis the early PK leader.

NFC West
NEW ORLEANS SAINTS
1989 Finish: Third
1990 Prediction: Fourth

John Fourcade   **Pat Swilling**

You figure the Saints out. We can't. Even coach Jim Mora can't figure out which team will show up on a given Sunday: the one that lost to the Rams and Lions when a playoff shot was on the line or the one who beat Buffalo, Philly, and Indianapolis to finish '89.

For starters there's QB John Fourcade (61 of 107, 930 yards, 7 TDs), the unknown soldier who came out of the bullpen to relieve Bobby Hebert (222 of 353, 2,686 yards, 15 TDs) for those final three victories. Can Fourcade get it done for an entire season? Major question for Mora.

RB Dalton Hilliard (344 rushes for 1,262 yards and 13 TDs), a 5–8 rock, is one of the NFL's best. If Rueben Mayes returns healthy, the Saints' running game will get even better. Huge FB Craig (Iron Head) Heyward (49 for 183) was rumored to be on the trading block.

WRs Lonzell Hill (48 catches for 636 yards) and Eric Martin (68 for 1,090) are adequate, with the jury still out on speedy Brett Perriman (20 for 356). TEs Hoby Brenner and John Tice do a decent job.

The play of rookie LT Kevin Haverdink was a pleasant surprise in '89, allowing Jim Dombrowski to move to LG for injured Brad Edelman. Joel Hilgenberg should return at C with aging RT Stan Brock and healthy-again RG Steve Trapilo.

Linebacking is the key to the New Orleans defense. ROLB Pat Swilling is one of the NFL's best (16½ sacks, fourth in the league) even after missing the entire '89 preseason. LOLB Rickey Jackson was first-rate after recovering from an auto-accident injury. Sam Mills and Vaughan Johnson are set on the inside.

Up front, gimpy James Geathers is gone (Plan B free agent), and LE Frank Warren and NT Jim Wilks are beginning to show their age. RE '89 rookie Wayne Martin should improve, but this unit is a major concern unless top pick Renaldo Turnbull comes through.

The loss of FS Dave Waymer (Plan B to San Francisco) hurts a little (too many bombs allowed), and RCB Toi Cook is shaky. Kim Phillips joins '89 rookie LCB Robert Massey and SS Gene Atkins.

Morten Andersen remains a premier PK.

The Colts gambled big-time that former
Illinois QB Jeff George, 1985's Gatorade HS
Player of the Year, is the real thing.

1990 NFL Draft List

The following abbreviations are used to identify the players' positions:

OFFENSE:
T = tackle; G = guard; C = center; QB = quarterback; RB = running back; WR = wide receiver; TE = tight end.

DEFENSE:
DE = defensive end; LB = linebacker; DT = defensive tackle; DB = defensive back.

SPECIAL TEAMS:
P = punter; K = placekicker.

The number before each player's name indicates the overall position in which he was drafted.

Atlanta Falcons

20. Steve Broussard, RB, Washington St.; 27. Darion Conner, LB, Jackson St.; 55. Oliver Barnett, DE, Kentucky; 121. Reggie Redding, TE, Fullerton St.; 139. Mike Pringle, LB, Fullerton St.; 195. Tony Epps, DT, Memphis St.; 222. Darrell Jordan, LB, No. Arizona; 278. Chris Ellison, DB, Houston; 305. Shawn McCarthy, P, Purdue.

Buffalo Bills

16. J.D. Williams, DB, Fresno St.; 42. Carwell Gardner, RB, Louisville; 69. Glenn Parker, T, Arizona; 100. Eddie Fuller, RB, LSU; 154. John Nies, P, Arizona; 166. Brent Griffith, G, Minnesota-Duluth; 170. Brent Collins, LB, Carson-Newman; 181. Fred DiRiggi, DT, Syracuse; 208. Marcus Patton, LB, UCLA; 238. Clarkston Hines, WR, Duke; 265. Mike Lodish, DT, UCLA; 292. Al Edwards, WR, Northwestern St.-Louisiana.

Chicago Bears

6. Mark Carrier, DB, USC; 32. Fred Washington, DT, TCU; 33. Ron Cox, LB, Fesno St.; 61. Tim Ryan, DT, USC; 64. Peter Tom Willis, QB, Florida St.; 88. Tony Moss, WR, LSU; 117. Pat Chaffey, RB, Oregon St.; 144. John Mangum, LB, Alabama; 176. Bill Anderson, G, Iowa; 200. James Rouse, RB, Arkansas; 228. James Bailey, RB, Texas A&M; 255. Terry Price, DT, Texas A&M; 284. Brent White, DT, Michigan; 298. Roman Matusz, T, Pittsburgh; 310. Anthony Cooney, DB, Arkansas.

Cincinnati Bengals

12. James Francis, LB, Baylor; 38. Harold Green, RB, So. Carolina; 65. Bernard Clark, LB, Miami; 92. Mike Brennan, T, Notre Dame; 123. Lynn James, WR, Arizona St.; 150. Don Odegard, DB, Nevada-Las Vegas; 177. Craig Ogletree, LB, Auburn; 204. Doug Wellsandt, TE, Washington St.; 234. Mitchell Price, DB, Tulane; 261. Eric Crigler, T, Murray St.; 288. Tim O'Connor, T, Virginia; 314. Andre Riley, WR, Washington.

Cleveland Browns

45. Leroy Hoardm, RB, Michigan; 73. Anthony Pleasant, DE, Tennessee St.; 101. Harlon Barnett, DB, Michigan St.; 129. Rob Burnett, DE, Syracuse; 157. Randy Hilliard, DB, Northwestern St.-Louisiana; 178. Scott Galbraith, TE, USC; 212. Jock Jones, LB, Virginia Tech; 240. Eugene Rowell, WR, So. Mississippi; 268. Michael Wallace, DB, Jackson St.; 296. Clemente Gordon, QB, Grambling; 323. Kerry Simlen, WR, Texas A&I.

Dallas Cowboys

17. Emmitt Smith, RB, Florida; 26. Alexander Wright, WR, Auburn; 63. Jimmie Jones, DE, Miami; 122. Stan Smagala, DB, Notre Dame; 221. Kenneth Gant, DB, Albany St.; 277. Dave Harper, LB, Humboldt St.

Denver Broncos

52. Alton Montgomery, DB, Houston; 82. Jerry Robinson, LB, Texas A&M; 111. Jeff Davidson, G, Ohio St.; 136. Le-Lo Lang, DB, Washington; 164. Ronnie Halliburton, TE, LSU; 192. Shannon Sharpe, WR, Savannah St.; 219. Brad Leggett, G, USC; 247. Todd Ellis, QB, So. Carolina; 275. Anthony Thompson, LB, E. Carolina.

Detroit Lions

7. Andre Ware, QB, Houston; 35. Dan Owens, DT, USC; 62. Mark Spindler, DT, Pitt; 91. Rob Hinckley, LB, Stanford; 105. Chris Oldham, DB, Oregon; 118. Jeff Campbell, WR, Colorado; 147. Maurice Henry, LB, Kansas St.; 174. Tracy Hayworth, LB, Tennessee; 194. Willie Green, WR, Mississippi; 203. Roman Fortin, G, San Diego St.; 229. Jack Linn, T, W. Virginia; 258. Bill Miller, WR, Illinois St.; 285. Reginald Wamsley, RB, So. Mississippi; 313. Robert Clayborn, WR, San Diego St.

Green Bay Packers

18. Tony Bennett, LB, Mississippi; 19. Darrell Thompson, RB, Minnesota; 48. Leroy Butler, DB, Florida St.; 75. Bobby Houston, LB, No. Carolina St.; 102. Jackie Harris, TE, NE Louisiana; 132. Charles Wilson, WR, Memphis St.; 159. Bryce Paup, LB, No. Iowa; 186. Lester Archambeau, DE, Stanford; 215. Roger Brown, DB, Virginia Tech; 242. Kim Baumgartner, QB, Wisconsin-Stevens Point; 269. Jerome Martin, DB, W. Kentucky; 299. Harry Jackson, RB, St. Cloud St.; 325. Kirk Maggio, P, UCLA.

Houston Oilers
15. Lamar Lathon, LB, Houston; 41. Jeff Alm, DT, Notre Dame; 72. Willis Peguese, DE, Miami; 99. Eric Still, G, Tennessee; 126. Richard Newbill, LB, Miami; 153. Tony Jones, WR, Texas; 184. Andy Murray, RB, Kentucky; 211. Brett Tucker, DB, No. Illinois; 237. Pat Coleman, WR, Mississippi; 264. Dee Thomas, DB, Nicholls, St.; 295. Joey Banes, T, Houston; 321. Reggie Slack, QB, Auburn.

Indianapolis Colts
1. Jeff George, QB, Illinois; 36. Anthony Johnson, RB, Notre Dame; 83. Stacey Simmons, WR, Florida; 94. Bill Schultz, G, USC; 103. Alan Grant, DB, Stanford; 106. Pat Cunningham, DT, Texas A&M; 148. Tony Walker, LB, SE Missouri St.; 179. James Singletary, LB, E. Carolina; 206. Ken Clark, RB, Nebraska; 213. Harvey Wilson, DB, Southern; 232. Darvell Huffman, WR, Boston Univ.; 290. Carnel Smith, DE, Pittsburgh; 311. Gene Benhart, QB, W. Illinois; 316, Dean Brown, T, Notre Dame.

Kansas City Chiefs
13. Percy Snow, LB, Michigan St.; 40. Tim Grunhard, C, Notre Dame; 96. Fred Jones, WR, Grambling; 124. Derrick Graham, T, Appalachian St.; 127. Ken Hackemack, DT, Texas; 152. Tony Sims, DB, Pittsburgh; 180. David Scott, G, Penn St.; 235. Michael Owens, LB, Syracuse; 263. Craig Hudson, TE, Wisconsin; 291. Ernest Thompson, RB, Georgia Southern; 318. Tony Jeffery, WR, San Jose St.

Los Angeles Raiders
11. Anthony Smith, DE, Arizona; 37. Aaron Wallace, LB, Texas A&M; 95. Torin Dorn, DB, North Carolina; 122. Stan Smagala, DB, Notre Dame; 149. Marcus Wilson, RB, Virginia; 173. Gary Lewis, DB, Alcorn St.; 197. Arthur Jimerson, DB, Norfolk St.; 230. Leon Perry, RB, Oklahoma; 259. James Szymanski, DE, Michigan St.; 303. Ron Lewis, WR, Jackson St.; 304. Myron Jones, RB, Fresno St.; 312. Major Harris, QB, W. Virginia; 331. Demetrius Davis, TE, Nevada-Reno.

Los Angeles Rams

23. Bern Brostek, C, Washington; 49. Pat Terrell, DB, Notre Dame; 78. Latin Berry, RB; Oregon; 161. Tim Stallworth, WR, Washington St.; 190. Kent Elmore, P, Tennessee; 198. Ray Savage, LB, Virginia; 216. Elbert Crawford, C, Arkansas; 245. Tony Lomack, WR, Florida; 272. Steven Bates, DE, James Madison; 301. Bill Goldberg, DT, Georgia; 327. David Lang, RB, No. Arizona.

Miami Dolphins

9. Richmond Webb, T, Texas A&M; 39. Keith Sims, T, Iowa St.; 66. Alfred Oglesby, DT, Houston; 93. Scott Mitchell, QB, Utah; 137. Leroy Holt, RB, USC; 151. Sean Vanhorse, DB,. Howard; 205. Thomas Woods, WR, Tennessee; 231. Phil Ross, TE, Oregon St.; 315. Bobby Harden, DB, Miami.

Minnesota Vikings

54. Mike Jones, TE, Texas A&M; 74. Marion Hobby, DE, Tennessee; 104. Alonzo Hampton, DB, Pittsburgh; 116. Reggie Thornton, WR, Bowling Green; 131. Cedric Smith, FB, Florida; 151. John Levelis, LB, C.W. Post; 205. Greg Schlichting, DE, Wyoming; 241. Terry Allen, RB, Clemson; 271. Donald Smith, DB, Liberty; 324. Ron Goetz, LB, Minnesota.

New England Patriots

8. Chris Singleton, LB, Arizona; 10. Ray Agnew, DE, No. Carolina St.; 59. Tom Hodson, QB, LSU; 80. Greg McMurtry, WR, Michigan; 110. Junior Robinson, DB, E. Carolina; 113. Jon Melander, T, Minnesota; 120. James Gray, RB, Texas Tech; 226. Shawn Bouwens, G, Nebraska Wesleyan; 253. Anthony Landry, RB, Stephen F. Austin; 280. Sean Smith, DE, Georgia Tech; 309. Ventson Donelson, DE, Michigan St.; 322. Blaine Rose, G, Maryland.

New Orleans Saints

14. Renaldo Turnbull, DE, W. Virginia; 44. Vince Buck, DB, Central St.; 71. Joel Smeenge, DE, W. Michigan; 98. DeMond Winston, LB, Vanderbilt; 125. Charles Arbuckle, TE, UCLA; 156. Mike Buck, QB, Maine; 158. James Williams, LB, Mississippi St.; 183. Scott Hough, G, Maine; 207. Jerry Gdowski, QB, Nebraska; 210. Derrick Carr, DE, Bowling Green; 233. Broderick Graves, RB, Winston Salem; 236. Lonnie Brockman, LB, W. Virginia; 260. Gary Cooper, WR, Clemson; 287. Webbie Burnett, DT, W. Kentucky; 320. Chris Port, G, Duke.

New York Giants

24. Rodney Hampton, RB, Georgia; 51. Mike Fox, DT, W. Virginia; 79. Greg Mark, DE, Miami; 107. David Whitmore, DB, Stephen F. Austin; 135. Craig Kupp, QB, Pacific Lutheran; 191. Aaron Emanuel, RB, USC; 218. Barry Voorhees, T, Cal St.-Northridge; 246. Clint James, DE, LSU; 274. Otis Moore, DT, Clemson; 302. Tim Downing, DE, Washington St.; 329. Matt Stover, K, Louisiana Tech.

New York Jets

2. Blair Thomas, RB, Penn St.; 28. Reggie Rembert, WR, W. Virginia; 56. Tony Stargell, DB, Tennessee St.; 84. Troy Taylor, QB, California; 112. Tony Savage, DT, Washington St.; 134. Robert McKnight, DB, TCU; 140. Terance Mills, WR, New Mexico; 167. Dwayne White, G, Alcorn St.; 168. Basil Proctor, LB, W. Virginia; 196. Roger Duffy, C, Penn St.; 223. Dale Dawkins, WR, Miami; 251. Brad Quast, LB, Iowa; 279. Derrick Kelson, DB, Purdue; 306. Darrell Davis, LB, TCU.

Philadelphia Eagles

22. Ben Smith, DB, Georgia; 50. Mike Bellamy, WR, Illinois; 77. Fred Barnett, WR, Arkansas St.; 133. Calvin Williams, WR, Purdue; 162. Kevin Thompson, DB, Oklahoma; 189. Terry Strouf, T, Wisconsin-LaCrosse; 217. Curt Dykes, T, Oregon; 244. Cecil Gray, DT, N. Carolina; 273. Orlando Adams, DT, Jacksonville; 294. John Hudson, C, Auburn; 300. Tyrone Watson, WR, Tennessee St.; 328. Judd Farrett, RB, Princeton.

Phoenix Cardinals

31. Anthony Thompson, RB, Indiana; 58. Richard Proehl, WR, Wake Forest; 85. Travis Davis, DT, Michigan St.; 115. Larry Centers, RB, Stephen F. Austin; 142. Tyrone Shavers, WR, Lamar; 169. Johnny Johnson, RB, San Jose St.; 199. Mickey Washington, DB, Texas A&M; 225. David Bavaro, LB, Syracuse; 252. Dave Elle, TE, So. Dakota; 282. Dempsey Norman, WR, St. Francis; 308. Donnie Riley, RB, Central Michigan; 330. Ken McMichael, LB, Oklahoma.

Pittsburgh Steelers

21. Eric Green, TE, Liberty; 43. Ken Davidson, DT, LSU; 70. Neil O'Donnell, QB, Maryland; 81. Craig Veasey, DT, Houston; 97. Chris Calloway, WR, Michigan; 128. Barry Foster, RB, Arkansas; 155. Ronald Heard, WR, Oregon; 192. Don Grayson, LB, Washington St.; 209. Karl Dunbar, DT, LSU; 239. Gary Jones, DB, Texas A&M; 266. Eddie Miles, LB, Minnesota; 293. Justin Strzelczyk, T, Maine; 319. Richard Bell, RB, Nebraska.

San Diego Chargers

5. Junior Seau, LB, USC; 57. Jeff Mills, LB, Nebraska; 60. Leo Goeas, G, Hawaii; 67. Walter Wilson, WR, E. Carolina; 138. John Friesz, QB, Idaho; 143. Frank Cornish, C, UCLA; 145. David Poole, DB, Carson-Newman; 163. Derrick Walker, TE, Michigan; 172. Jeff Novak, G, SW Texas St.; 185. Joe Staysniak, T, Ohio St.; 197. Nathaniel Lewis, WR, Oregon Tech; 193. Keith Collins, DB, Appalachian St.; 201. J.J. Flannigan, RB, Colorado; 227. Chris Goetz, G, Pittsburgh; 256. Kenny Berry, DB, Miami; 283. Tommy Stowers, TE, Missouri; 326. Elliott Searcy, WR, Southern.

San Francisco 49ers

25. Dexter Carter, RB, Florida St.; 47. Dennis Brown, DT, Washintgon; 53. Eric Davis, DB, Jacksonville; 68. Ron Lewis, WR, Florida St.; 89. Dean Caliguire, C, Pittsburgh; 165. Frank Pollack, T, No. Arizona; 220. Dwight Pickens, WR, Fresno St.; 248. Odell Haggins, DT, Florida St.; 276. Martin Harrison, DE, Washington; 289. Anthony Shelton, DB, Tennessee St.

Seattle Seahawks

3. Cortez Kennedy, DT, Miami; 29. Terry Wooden, LB, Syracuse; 34. Robert Blackmon, DB, Baylor; 90. Chris Warren, RB, Ferrum; 119. Eric Hayes, DT, Florida St.; 146. Ned Bolcar, LB, Notre Dame; 175. Bob Kula, T, Michigan St.; 202. Bill Hitchcock, T, Purdue; 257. Robert Morris, DE, Valdosta St.; 286. Darryl Reed, DB, Oregon; 312. John Gromos, QB, Vanderbilt.

Tampa Bay Buccaneers

4. Keith McCants, LB, Alabama; 30. Reggie Cobb, RB, Tennessee; 87. Jesse Anderson, TE, Mississippi St.; 114. Ian Beckles, G, Indiana; 141. Derrick Douglass, RB, Louisiana Tech; 171. Donnie Gardner, DE, Kentucky; 224. Terry Cook, DE, Fresno St.; 254. Mike Busch, TE, Iowa St.; 281. Terry Anthony, WR, Florida St.; 307. Todd Hammel, QB, Stephen F. Austin.

Washington Redskins

46. Andre Collins, LB, Penn St.; 76. Mohammed Elewonibi, G, Brigham Young; 86. Cary Conklin, QB, Washington; 109. Rico Labbe, DB, Boston Col.; 130. Brian Mitchell, RB, SW Louisiana; 160. Kent Wells, DB, Nebraska; 243. Tim Moxley, G, Ohio St.; 262. D'Juan Francisco, DB, Notre Dame; 270. Thomas Rayam, DT, Alabama; 297. Jon Leverenz, LB, Minnesota.

1989 Statistics

Leading Rushers	Att.	Yards	Avg.	TDs
AFC				
Okoye, K.C.	370	1480	4.0	12
Dickerson, Ind.	314	1311	4.2	7
Thomas, Buff.	298	1244	4.2	▓
Brooks, Cin.	221	1239	5.6	▓
Humphrey, Den.	294	1151	3.9	7
Jackson, Raiders	173	950	5.5	4
Stephens, N.E.	244	833	3.4	7
Worley, Pitt.	195	770	3.9	5
Hector, Jets	177	702	4.0	3
Butts, S.D.	170	683	4.0	9
Smith, Mia.	200	659	3.3	6
Metcalf, Clev.	187	633	3.4	6
Warner, Sea.	194	631	3.3	3
Hoge, Pitt.	186	621	3.3	8
Perryman, N.E.	150	562	3.7	2
Kinnebrew, Buff.	131	533	4.1	6
Highsmith, Hou.	128	531	4.1	4
Spencer, S.D.	134	521	3.9	3
Williams, Sea.	146	499	3.4	1
Smith, Raiders	117	471	4.0	1

Leading Rushers	Att.	Yards	Avg.	TDs
NFC				
Sanders, Det.	280	1470	5.3	14
Anderson, Chi.	274	1275	4.7	11
Hilliard, N.O.	344	1262	3.7	13
Bell, Rams	272	1137	4.2	15
Craig, S.F.	271	1054	3.9	6
Anderson, Giants	325	1023	3.1	14
Walker, Dall.-Minn.	250	915	3.7	7
Riggs, Wash.	201	834	4.1	4
Fullwood, G.B.	204	821	4.0	5
Settle, Atl.	179	689	3.8	3
Cunningham, Phil.	104	621	6.0	4
Tate, T.B.	167	589	3.5	8
Fenney, Minn.	151	588	3.9	4
Toney, Phil.	172	582	3.4	3
Byner, Wash.	134	580	4.3	7
Ferrell, Phoe.	149	502	3.4	6
Byars, Phil.	133	452	3.4	5
Palmer, Dall.	112	446	4.0	2

Leading Passers	Att.	Comp.	Yds. Gnd.	TD Pass	Int.	Rating
AFC						
Esiason, Cin.	455	258	3525	28	11	92.1
Moon, Hou.	464	280	3631	23	14	88.9
Kelly, Buff.	391	228	3130	25	18	86.2
Kosar, Clev.	513	303	3533	18	14	80.3
Marino, Mia.	550	308	3997	24	22	76.9
DeBerg, K.C.	324	196	2529	11	16	75.8
Krieg, Sea.	499	286	3309	21	20	74.8
O'Brien, Jets	477	288	3346	12	18	74.3
Elway, Den.	416	223	3051	18	18	73.7
McMahon, S.D.	318	176	2132	10	10	73.5
Brister, Pitt.	342	187	2365	9	10	73.1
Trudeau, Ind.	362	190	2317	15	13	71.3
Grogan, N.E.	261	133	1697	9	14	60.8

Leading Passers	Att.	Comp.	Yds. Gnd.	TD Pass	Int.	Rat- ing
NFC						
Montana, S.F.	396	271	3521	26	8	112.4
Everett, Rams	518	304	4310	29	17	90.6
Rypien, Wash.	476	280	3768	22	13	88.1
Hebert, N.O.	353	222	2686	15	15	82.7
Majkowski, G.B.	599	353	4318	27	20	82.3
Simms, Giants	405	228	3061	14	14	77.6
Miller, Atl.	526	280	3459	16	10	76.1
Cunningham, Phil.	532	290	3400	21	15	75.5
Wilson, Minn.	362	194	2543	9	12	70.5
Hogeboom, Phoe.	364	204	2591	14	19	69.5
Testaverde, T.B.	480	258	3133	20	22	68.9
Tomczak, Chi.	306	156	2058	16	16	68.2
Gagliano, Det.	232	117	1671	6	12	61.2
Aikman, Dall.	293	155	1749	9	18	55.7

Leading Receivers	No.	Yards	Avg.	TDs
AFC				
Reed, Buff.	88	1312	14.9	
Blades, Sea.	77	1063	13.8	
Johnson, Den.	76	1095	14.4	7
Williams, Sea.	76	657	8.6	6
Miller, S.D.	75	1252	16.7	10
Hill, Hou.	66	938	14.2	8
Slaughter, Clev.	65	1236	19.0	6
McGee, Cin.	65	1211	18.6	8
Clayton, Mia.	64	1011	15.8	9
Brooks, Ind.	63	919	14.6	4
Toon, Jets	63	693	11.0	2
Jensen, Mia.	61	557	9.1	6
Langhorne, Clev.	60	749	12.5	2
Thomas, Buff.	60	669	11.2	6
Fernandez, Raiders	57	1069	18.8	9
Givins, Hou.	55	794	14.4	3
Sievers, N.E.	54	615	11.4	0

Leading Receivers	No.	Yards	Avg.	TDs
NFC				
Sharpe, G.B.	90	1423	15.8	12
Carrier, T.B.	86	1422	16.5	9
Monk, Wash.	86	1186	13.8	8
Rice, S.F.	82	1483	18.1	17
Sanders, Wash.	80	1138	14.2	4
Clark, Wash.	79	1229	15.6	9
Rathman, S.F.	73	616	8.4	1
Ellard, Rams	70	1382	19.7	8
Johnson, Det.	70	1091	15.6	8
Martin, N.O.	68	1090	16.0	8
Byars, Phil.	68	721	10.6	0
Carter, Minn.	65	1066	16.4	4
Jackson, Phil.	63	648	10.3	3
Smith, Phoe.	62	778	12.5	5
Taylor, S.F.	60	1077	18.0	10
Woodside, G.B.	59	527	8.9	0
Collions, Atl.	58	862	14.9	3

ding Interceptors	No.	Yards	Long	TDs
Wright, Clev.	9	91	27	1
Fulcher, Cin.	8	87	22	0
Taylor, Ind.	7	225	80	1
Byrd, S.D.	7	38	22	0
McMillan, Jets	6	180	92	1
Braxton, Den.	6	103	34	1
Kelso, Buff.	6	101	43	0
NFC				
Allen, Phil.	8	38	18	0
McDonald, Phoe.	7	170	53	1
Holmes, Det.	6	77	36	1
Hamilton, T.B.	6	70	30	0
Waymer, N.O.	6	66	42	0
Gray, Rams	6	48	27	1
Robinson, T.B.	6	44	16	0

Leading Scorers, Kicking	XP	XPA	FG	FGA	TP
AFC					
Treadwell, Den.	39	40	27	33	120
Norwood, Buff.	46	47	23	30	115
Zendejas, Hou.	40	40	25	37	115
Lowery, K.C.	34	35	24	33	106
Jaeger, Raiders	34	34	23	34	103
Stoyanovich, Mia.	38	39	19	26	95
Biasucci, Ind.	31	32	21	27	94
Anderson, Pitt.	28	28	21	30	91
NFC					
Cofer, S.F.	49	51	29	36	136
Lohmiller, Wash.	41	41	29	40	128
Karlis, Minn.	27	28	31	39	120
Lansford, Rams	51	51	23	30	120
Jacke, G.B.	42	42	22	28	108
Andersen, N.O.	44	45	20	29	104
Igwebuike, T.B.	33	35	22	28	99
Murray, Det.	36	36	20	21	96

Leading Scorers, Touchdowns	TDs	Rush	Rec.	Ret.	
AFC					
Okoye, K.C.	12	12	0	0	72
Thomas, Buff.	12	6	6	0	72
Miller, S.D.	11	0	10	1	66
Metcalf, Clev.	10	6	4	0	60
Brooks, Cin.	9	7	2	0	54
Butts, S.D.	9	9	0	0	54
Clayton, Mia.	9	0	9	0	54
Fernandez, Raiders	9	0	9	0	54
Holman, Cin.	9	0	9	0	54
Reed, Buff.	9	0	9	0	54
Dickerson, Ind.	8	7	1	0	48
Hill, Hou.	8	0	8	0	48
Hoge, Pitt.	8	8	0	0	48
Humphrey, Den.	8	7	1	0	48
McGee, Cin.	8	0	8	0	48

Leading Scorers, Touchdowns	TDs	Rush	Rec.	Ret.	TP
NFC					
Hilliard, N.O.	18	13	5	0	108
Rice, S.F.	17	0	17	0	102
Anderson, Chi.	15	11	4	0	90
Bell, Rams	15	15	0	0	90
Anderson, Giants	14	14	0	0	84
Sanders, Det.	14	14	0	0	84
Sharpe, G.B.	13	0	12	1	78
Carter, Phil.	11	0	11	0	66
Taylor, S.F.	10	0	10	0	60
Walker, Dall.-Minn.	10	7	2	1	60
Byner, Wash.	9	7	2	0	54
Carrier, T.B.	9	0	9	0	54
Clark, Wash.	9	0	9	0	54
Tate, T.B.	9	8	1	0	54
Ellard, Rams	8	0	8	0	48
Johnson, Det.	8	0	8	0	48
Martin, N.O.	8	0	8	0	48
Monk, Wash.	8	0	8	0	48
......ter, Chi.	8	5	3	0	48

Leading Punters	No.	Yards	Long	Avg.
AFC				
Montgomery, Hou.	56	2422	63	43.3
Stark, Ind.	79	3392	64	42.9
Roby, Mia.	58	2458	58	42.4
Newsome, Pitt.	82	3368	57	41.1
Gossett, Raiders	67	2711	60	40.5
Horan, Den.	77	3111	63	40.4
Goodburn, K.C.	67	2688	54	40.1
Ilesic, S.D.	76	3049	64	40.1
Johnson, Cin.	61	2446	62	40.1
Rodriguez, Sea.	75	2995	59	39.9
Kidd, Buff.	65	2564	60	39.4
Prokop, Jets	87	3426	76	39.4
Wagner, Clev.	97	3817	60	39.4

Leading Punters	No.	Yards	Long	Avg.
NFC				
Camarillo, Phoe.	76	3298	58	43.4
Arnold, Det.	82	3538	64	43.1
Landeta, Giants	70	3019	71	43.1
Mojsiejenko, Wash.	62	2663	74	43.0
Fulhage, Atl.	84	3472	65	41.3
Saxon, Dall.	79	3233	56	40.9
Bracken, G.B.	66	2682	63	40.6
Helton, S.F.	55	2226	56	40.5
Scribner, Minn.	72	2864	55	39.8
Barnhardt, N.O.	55	2179	56	39.6
Buford, Chi.	72	2844	60	39.5
Mohr, T.B.	84	3311	58	39.4

Leading Punt Returners	No.	Yards	Avg.	TDs
AFC				
Verdin, Ind.	23	296	12.9	1
McNeil, Clev.	49	496	10.1	0
Townsell, Jets	33	299	9.1	0
Sutton, G.B.-Buff.	31	273	8.8	
Woodson, Pitt.	29	207	7.1	
Bell, Den.	21	143	6.8	0
NFC				
Stanley, Det.	36	496	13.8	0
Meggett, Giants	46	582	12.7	1
Sikahema, Phoe.	37	433	11.7	0
Taylor, S.F.	36	417	11.6	0
Drewrey, T.B.	20	220	11.0	0
Sanders, Atl.	28	307	11.0	1
Lewis, Minn.	44	446	10.1	0
Howard, Wash.	21	200	9.5	0
Henley, Rams	28	266	9.5	0
Williams, Phil.	30	267	8.9	0
Query, G.B.	30	247	8.2	0
Shepard, N.O.-Dall.	31	251	8.1	1
Harris, N.O.	27	196	7.3	0

Leading Kickoff Returners	No.	Yards	Avg.	TDs
AFC				
Woodson, Pitt.	36	982	27.3	1
Logan, Mia.	24	613	25.5	1
Miller, S.D.	21	533	25.4	1
Martin, N.E.	24	584	24.3	0
Jefferson, Sea.	22	511	23.2	1
Metcalf, Clev.	31	718	23.2	0
Jennings, Cin.	26	525	20.2	0
Bell, Den.	30	602	20.1	0
Adams, Raiders	22	425	19.3	0
Townsell, Jets	34	653	19.2	0
Tucker, Buff.-N.E.	23	436	19.0	0
Copeland, K.C.	26	466	17.9	0
Johnson, Hou.	21	372	17.7	0
Holland, S.D.	29	510	17.6	0
Humphery, Jets	24	414	17.3	0
NFC				
Gray, Det.	24	640	26.7	0
Dixon, Dall.	47	1181	25.1	1
...rd, Wash.	21	522	24.9	1
...y, Chi.	28	667	23.8	0
Meggett, Giants	27	577	21.4	0
Sanders, Chi.	23	491	21.3	1
Johnson, Wash.	24	504	21.0	0
Sanders, Atl.	35	725	20.7	0
Brown, Rams	47	968	20.6	0
Sikahema, Phoe.	43	874	20.3	0
Flagler, S.F.	32	643	20.1	0
Shepard, N.O.-Dall.	27	529	19.6	0
Jones, Atl.	23	440	19.1	0
Usher, S.D.-Phoe.	27	506	18.7	0
Elder, T.B.	40	685	17.1	0
Workman, G.B.	33	547	16.6	0
Ingram, Giants	22	332	15.1	0

1990
NFL Schedule

Sunday, September 9
Indianapolis at Buffalo
N.Y. Jets at Cincinnati
Pittsburgh at Cleveland
Denver at L.A. Raiders
Houston at Atlanta
Minnesota at Kansas City
Miami at New England
San Diego at Dallas
Seattle at Chicago
Green Bay at L.A. Rams
Phil. at N.Y. Giants
Phoenix at Washington
Tampa Bay at Detroit

Monday, September 10
San Fran. at New Orleans

Sunday, September 16
Buffalo at Miami
Cincinnati at San Diego
Cleveland at N.Y. Jets
Houston at Pittsburgh
New Eng. at Indianapolis
L.A. Raiders at Seattle
Atlanta at Detroit
Chicago at Green Bay
N.Y. Giants at Dallas
L.A. Rams at Tampa Bay
New Orleans at Minnesota
Phoenix at Philadelphia
Washington at San Fran.

Monday, September 17
Kansas City at Denver

Sunday, September 23
New England at Cincinnati
San Diego at Cleveland
Seattle at Denver
Indianapolis at Houston
Kansas City at Green Bay
Pitt. at L.A. Raiders
Miami at N.Y. Giants
Atlanta at San Francisco
Minnesota at Chicago
Dallas at Washington
Detroit at Tampa Bay
Philadelphia at L.A. R
Phoenix at New Orle

Monday, September 24
Buffalo at N.Y. Jets

Sunday, September 30
Denver at Buffalo
Cleveland at Kansas City
Houston at San Diego
Indianapolis at Phila.
Chicago at L.A. Raiders
Miami at Pittsburgh
N.Y. Jets at New England
Dallas at N.Y. Giants
Green Bay at Detroit
Tampa Bay at Minnesota
Washington at Phoenix

Monday, October 1
Cincinnati at Seattle

Sunday, October 7
L.A. Raiders at Buffalo
Cincinnati at L.A. Rams
San Francisco at Houston
Kan. City at Indianapolis
N.Y. Jets at Miami
Seattle at New England
San Diego at Pittsburgh
New Orleans at Atlanta
Green Bay at Chicago
Tampa Bay at Dallas
Detroit at Minnesota

Monday, October 8
Cleveland at Denver

Sunday, October 14
Houston at Cincinnati
Cleveland at New Orleans
Pittsburgh at Denver
▓▓▓ at Kansas City
▓▓ at L.A. Raiders
San Diego at N.Y. Jets
San Francisco at Atlanta
L.A. Rams at Chicago
Dallas at Phoenix
Green Bay at Tampa Bay
N.Y. Giants at Washington

Monday, October 15
Minnesota at Philadelphia

Thursday, October 18
New England at Miami

Sunday, October 21
N.Y. Jets at Buffalo
Denver at Indianapolis
New Orleans at Houston
Kansas City at Seattle
L.A. Raiders at San Diego
Pittsburgh at San Fran.
Atlanta at L.A. Rams
Dallas at Tampa Bay
Phoenix at N.Y. Giants
Philadelphia at Wash.

Monday, October 22
Cincinnati at Cleveland

Sunday, October 28
Buffalo at New England
Cincinnati at Atlanta
Cleveland at San Fran.
N.Y. Jets at Houston
Miami at Indianapolis
Tampa Bay at San Diego
Chicago at Phoenix
Philadelphia at Dallas
Detroit at New Orleans
Minnesota vs. Green Bay
   at Milwaukee
Washington at N.Y. Giants

Monday, October 29
L.A. Rams at Pittsburgh

Sunday, November 4
Buffalo at Cleveland
New Orleans at Cincinnati
Denver at Minnesota
Houston at L.A. Rams
L.A. Raiders at Kan. City
Phoenix at Miami
New Eng. at Philadelphia
Dallas at N.Y. Jets
Atlanta at Pittsburgh
San Diego at Seattle
Chicago at Tampa Bay
Washington at Detroit
San Fran. at Green Bay

Monday, November 5
N.Y. Giants at Indianap.

Sunday, November 11
Phoenix at Buffalo
Denver at San Diego
Indianap. at New England
Seattle at Kansas City
Green Bay at L.A. Raiders
Miami at N.Y. Jets
Atlanta at Chicago
San Francisco at Dallas
Minnesota at Detroit
N.Y. Giants at L.A. Rams
Tampa Bay at New Orl.

Monday, November 12
Wash. at Philadelphia

Sunday, November 18
New England at Buffalo
Houston at Cleveland
Chicago at Denver
N.Y. Jets at Indianapolis
Pittsburgh at Cincinnati
San Diego at Kansas City
Minnesota at Seattle
Philadelphia at Atlanta
Dallas at L.A. Rams
Detroit at N.Y. Giants
Green Bay at Phoenix
New Orleans at Wash.
Tampa Bay at San Fran.

Monday, November 19
L.A. Raiders at Miami

Thursday, November 22
Denver at Detroit
Washington at Dallas

Sunday, November 25
Indianapolis at Cin.
Miami at Cleveland
Kan. City at L.A. Raiders
New England at Phoenix
Pittsburgh at N.Y. Jets
Seattle at San Diego
Atlanta at New Orleans
Chicago at Minnesota
Tampa Bay vs. Green Bay
   at Milwaukee
L.A. Rams at San Fran.
N.Y. Giants at Phil.

Monday, November 26
Buffalo at Houston

Sunday, December 2
Philadelphia at Buffalo
Cincinnati at Pittsburgh
L.A. Rams at Cleveland
L.A. Raiders at Denver
Houston at Seattle
Indianapolis at Phoenix
Kan. City at New England
Miami at Washington
N.Y. Jets at San Diego
Atlanta at Tampa Bay
Detroit at Chicago
New Orleans at Dallas
Green Bay at Minnesota

Monday, December 3
N.Y. Giants at San Fran.

Sunday, December 9
Buffalo at Indianapolis
Cleveland at Houston
Denver at Kansas City
Philadelphia at Miami
New England at Pittsburgh

Seattle vs. Green Bay
   at Milwaukee
Phoenix at Atlanta
Chicago at Washington
New Orleans at L.A. Rams
Minnesota at N.Y. Giants
San Fran. at Cincinnati

Monday, December 10
L.A. Raiders at Detroit

Saturday, December 15
Wash. at New England
Buffalo at N.Y. Giants

Sunday, December 16
Cin. at L.A. Raiders
Atlanta at Cleveland
San Diego at Denver
Houston at Kansas City
Indianapolis at N.Y. Jets
Seattle at Miami
Pittsburgh at New Orleans
[illegible] at Detroit
[illegible] at Dallas
Green Bay at Philadelphia
Minnesota at Tampa Bay

Monday, December 17
San Fran. at L.A. Rams

Saturday, December 22
L.A. Raiders at Minnesota
Detroit at Green Bay
Wash. at Indianapolis

Sunday, December 23
Miami at Buffalo
Cincinnati at Houston
Cleveland at Pittsburgh
Kansas City at San Diego
New England at N.Y. Jets
L.A. Rams at Atlanta
Tampa Bay at Chicago
Dallas at Philadelphia
New Orleans at San Fran.
N.Y. Giants at Phoenix
Denver at Seattle

Saturday, December 29
Philadelphia at Phoenix
Kansas City at Chicago

Sunday, December 30
Buffalo at Washington
Cleveland at Cincinnati
Green Bay at Denver
Pittsburgh at Houston
Indianapolis at Miami
San Diego at L.A. Raiders
Detroit at Seattle
Dallas at Atlanta
San Fran. at Minnesota
N.Y. Giants at New Eng.
N.Y. Jets at Tampa Bay

Monday, December 31
L.A. Rams at New Orleans

BRUCE WEBER PICKS
HOW THEY'LL FINISH IN 1990

AFC East
1. Miami
2. Buffalo
3. New England
4. Indianapolis
5. N.Y. Jets

AFC Central
1. Pittsburgh
2. Cincinnati
3. Houston
4. Cleveland

AFC West
1. Kansas City
2. Denver
3. L.A. Raiders
4. San Diego
5. Seattle

NFC East
1. N.Y. Giants
2. Philadelphia
3. Washington
4. Dallas
5. Phoenix

NFC Central
1. Green Bay
2. Detroit
3. Minnesota
4. Chicago
5. Tampa Bay

NFC West
1. San Francisco
2. L.A. Rams
3. Atlanta
4. New Orleans

Wild Cards: Cincinnati, Denver, Houston;
Philadelphia, L.A. Rams, Washington

AFC Champions: Pittsburgh
NFC Champions: San Francisco
Super Bowl Champions: San Francisco (yes, again!)

YOU PICK
HOW THEY'LL FINISH IN 1990

AFC East

1.
2.
3.
4.
5.

AFC Central

1.
2.
3.

AFC West

1.
2.
3.
4.
5.

NFC East

1.
2.
3.
4.
5.

NFC Central

1.
2.
3.
4.
5.

NFC West

1.
2.
3.
4.

Wild Cards:

AFC Champions:

NFC Champions:

Super Bowl Champions: